THREE PHASES OF EVENTING

⋄ *EVENTING* ⋄
PREPARATION, TRAINING & COMPETITION

Judy Bradwell

with Claude Keith

The Crowood Press

First published in 1988 by
The Crowood Press
Ramsbury, Marlborough,
Wiltshire SN8 2HE

British Library Cataloguing in Publication Data

Bradwell, Judy
    Eventing — Preparation, Training and Competition
    1. Eventing
    I. Title
    798.2′4

ISBN 1 85223 033 9

All photographs taken by Kit Houghton
Line drawings by Elaine Roberts

Typeset by Alacrity Phototypesetters, Weston-super-Mare
Printed in Great Britain by Butler & Tanner Ltd, Frome and London

Contents

Acknowledgements

This book is dedicated to my father, Mr Bill Bradwell, whose unending support has made my success possible. Whether it has been a bleak late autumn day, a glorious summer day, or hundreds of miles from home, 'Mr Bradwell' has always been there. Many of my good horses he has found inexpensively on his quiet forages around the country. He has never interfered with or criticised my riding, but has often made constructive comments about the way the horses have gone.

The photographs in this book have all been taken by Kit Houghton, and most of them deliberately feature young horses in my yard — High Renown, a six-year-old dark brown gelding, Foxy V, a seven-year-old chestnut gelding, and High Risk, a ten-year-old gelding, used to show the more advanced movements at dressage.

The pupil featured is Christine Wallner from California, USA.

Introduction

This book is written for all those people who, like myself, have had a yearning to succeed in the world of equestrianism. Whether you start out young or old, or are having to restart after injury (as I did), the discipline, the dedication and the will to win must all be there in earnest. There are no short cuts, no easy routes to success and no ways of disguising problems. It takes hard work, long hours, great preparation and, above all, a true partnership based on mutual respect between horse and rider to achieve the highs that this sport can provide.

I have chosen to write this book while I am still, even after twenty-five years, getting up early most days and riding five to seven horses before lunch. This means that its contents are based on my own current experiences. It reflects my continuing respect for the sport I love – respect born out of the fact that it is only through understanding that knowledge can be acquired and it is this knowledge that establishes the partnership I possess with each horse I ride. No one horse is ever the same as the next. Each requires personal attention to tack, to feed, to exercise, to interest and to competition.

Eventing has been, for me, the supreme test of horse and rider, combining the control and obedience of dressage with the challenge and excitement of cross country, and culminating in the precision required for show jumping. I am proud to have represented my country and to have ridden great horses like Castlewellan, William Hinckling, Justin Time, Don Camillo, and Derby House. I have also been fortunate enough to have won many of the great and long-established Horse Trials competitions in Great Britain. Most importantly perhaps, I have made great friends the world over from people brought together in competition, who transcend that and have a mutual respect and admiration.

However, before you run away with the idea that it has all gone right for me, I should relate that in February 1981 my career seemed to be over, due to a freak hunting accident. The injury I sustained crushed the nerves in my left leg and the doctor's diagnosis was that I would never ride again, let alone compete. It took me three years to get back to eventing, but in the late spring of 1984 I was able to compete at Wingerworth on a five-year-old, High Risk, and won a Novice Class. That was where my dedication, hard work and competitive spirit, plus the support of a number of close friends, really came to fruition. The will to win can overcome most adversities and if you have the talent and want success badly enough it can be achieved. What this book does, I hope, is to provide you with an insight into what you have to do, learn and look for, so that eventually it becomes second nature. One thing I have learned over the years is that you have to put a lot of hard work into the sport to get anything out of it.

Finally, remember that preparation, discipline, commitment and patience bring results. If it is any consolation, quite apart from the hours I spend alone working with my team of horses, I still take lessons in dressage and show jumping to improve my performance and technique, while hopefully getting the most out of my horses. You must never stop learning, and fortunately there is always room for improvement and plenty of variety in this exacting sport.

1 Selecting and Buying the Right Horse

Many parallels are drawn between the motor car and the horse, especially as both have four corners, and are admired for their performance, handling and appearance. However, there is one fundamental difference – the horse is a living being, the car a mechanical construction. As such, while both respond to careful maintenance throughout the year, the horse reacts to individuals and, if not carefully looked after, can become unhappy, lazy, listless, bored and even obstinate. Like a human being, the horse reacts to different people and environments and this needs to be taken into account when looking to buy a horse.

The well-known advertising slogan used for the Ford Fiesta motor car – 'Man and his machine in perfect harmony' – is never more appropriate than when applied to the relationship struck up between horse and rider seeking to make it to the top. To achieve this harmony the height, weight and riding style of the rider have to be taken into account when looking for the optimum ride. Most of the top event riders tend to have a certain stamp of a horse that they prefer to ride, and this has a lot to do with what they were used to riding when they were younger and which horses play to their strengths as a horseman. There are always exceptions: the Los Angeles Olympic Champion Mark Todd is over 6ft 3in, but has still ridden the 15.3hh. brown gelding Charisma to great effect,

even if, at first sight, they look an unlikely combination.

Not surprisingly, most starters in the sport of eventing tend to be young enthusiasts from families with limited funds available to invest in what could be a passing phase. This means that, over time, they either grow out of their horse in the pursuit of the sport, or lose interest. Many horses are bought by parents simply because they are liked, considered to be safe or just happen to be on offer. These circumstances are not necessarily bad, as they can often help a rider to find out what type of horse will eventually suit him best as he becomes more accomplished and expert.

There are, however, many aspects to consider before spending money on what is inevitably going to be a heavy financial drain. Horses are never cheap – it is not the purchase price that is the major factor but the upkeep and running costs. The age of the horse is critical. If the rider wants to progress quickly then an older horse of around eight to ten years will be preferable to a two- or three-year-old who will not even be allowed to go eventing until he is five. There are, of course, advantages in taking a young horse and bringing it on. It will tend to be less expensive initially, and horse and rider can be trained together, avoiding the bad habits a horse may have got used to under a previous owner, who was perhaps uninspired or non-competitive.

What to Look For

Soundness

The sport of eventing is extremely taxing for a horse and it is for this reason that a number of critical facets must be sought and assessed. Soundness is essential – if there is any history of lameness, leg problems or radiological disfigurements, or if you just have a gut feeling about it, don't even consider the purchase. The likelihood is that the horse will not be able to take the strain of the work that has to go into preparing him for competition. Furthermore, even if he seems sound at the time of viewing and trial, the chances are that a horse with a history will only go so far before his limitations are exposed – this often happens, with sad and disastrous consequences to the animal. The correct procedure is to have the horse thoroughly vetted by a reputable vet, who will carry out feet X-rays, and scrutinise and, where relevant, discuss any veterinary records.

Temperament

Temperament is almost as important as soundness – if the horse is not generous, he will not be able to concentrate or give of his best to the rider, either during the training or at the events themselves. You need to look for a positive attitude from the horse and an acceptance and enjoyment of schooling and working. The horse should be willing to please and to learn, and content to be alone, or to leave home and be stabled in an unfamiliar setting. Questions about his attitude in the past should always be asked.

It should, however, be clearly understood that a horse who has been used to one yard will take time to settle into a new home, and a few difficulties should be expected. Given patience, understanding and, ideally, the chance to be turned out for a while each day as well as being ridden, the horse should settle into his new quarters within a week.

A 'nappy' horse is one that resists or is reluctant to leave the company of other horses in the yard. He should be avoided because he will be unwilling to co-operate with the rider's instructions. Importantly, reject an excitable horse as this often suggests a bad temperament and, more often than not, the event will be over before it begins should the horse get really worked up on the day. There is always the danger with a 'hot horse' that

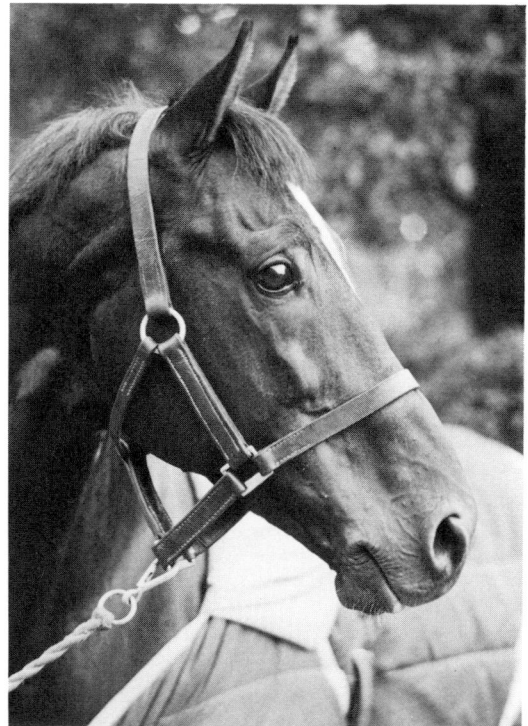

Fig 1   A kind and intelligent eye.

he can get too excited in the dressage phase, eagerly anticipating the jumps on the cross country, often in blind panic and with proven misjudgement.

Much can be told from the eye. It should be kind and alive but not wild. If it is too dead then the horse may be too casual and incapable of rising to the occasion. If he has a mean or a 'piggy' eye this is often an indication of a horse with an ungenerous nature. In this respect horses are no different from humans and, while there are always exceptions, the eye is often a good indicator.

Movement

It is very important that the horse should have inherently good movement. Contrary to popular belief, movement can only be improved to a limited extent with training, and if it is not part of the horse's natural make-up he will struggle to make the grade. A good mover is a horse who is light on his feet and has three good paces – walk, trot and gallop. He should also be able to lengthen his stride in trot and gallop. It is not only in the dressage phase that good paces and movement are essential, but also on the cross country – a naturally good mover will tend to be lighter in his action and better balanced. These assets will enable the horse to withstand the wear and tear from jumping and galloping on the different terrains encountered around the country.

Boldness

The horse you select for eventing must be bold and athletic. Boldness in an eventer means not being afraid and having a positive approach when encountering ditches and water obstacles. This has nothing to do with size as many small horses have big hearts; indeed, with courses having changed to feature more combinations and bounces, you will often find a smaller horse is better suited to these more technical types of fence.

Being athletic simply means that the horse should neither hang nor dangle his front legs when he jumps, should enjoy jumping and must be able both to stand off or get in close and shorten or lengthen his stride pattern accordingly. This is all much more important than the ability to jump big and carefully, as this might indicate the horse would be better suited to show jumping rather than eventing.

A fine example of a bold and athletic jumper in the event world has been Lucinda Green's brown gelding Regal Realm, who, after completing Burghley in 1987 and being placed, was retired at the age of fifteen. In his illustrious career Regal Realm competed in numerous three day events, winning both major championships and International honours.

Conformation

Conformation is important for an eventer and is often closely allied to soundness. Naturally, the first thing to decide when you see a new horse is whether or not he appeals to you. If he does then you must decide whether the horse is a good colour. Many equestrian people express a particular preference for a good bay, bright or dark, brown, liver chestnut, or a good grey. The old adage 'a good horse is never a bad colour' tends to be true. Next consider the eye, which should be big and bold and set well forward in the head, giving a good, kind, willing and generous expression. The horse should cock its ears and come across as having character. First impressions will normally be correct, so do look for the good bold eye, the flat forehead between the eyes, big ears set wide apart, and a big wide nostril not set too low.

When the mouth is opened, the front incisor teeth should meet exactly together and the molars (the teeth at the back of the head) should be set as far back as possible. If the latter are not in the right place then a snaffle bit will not be able to be worn, because when ridden it will have a nut-cracker effect, coming directly into contact with the first molars, and will be very uncomfortable for the horse. Check for wolf teeth, which are small sharp teeth that form directly in front of the molars and which, if not extracted when fully formed, can cause trouble.

A good horse should have plenty of room underneath his throat. A good test is to put your clenched fist under the throat, where there should neither be tightness nor restriction. The neck itself should be well set on at both ends. At the top end you should be able to put at least two fingers where the neck joins the head. The top line of the neck should have a good length to it, while the mane must be long enough to allow between nine and twelve plaits in it. The underline should not be too short. The shoulder itself should be deep, set in the form of a triangle, and have a well-formed wither.

The foreleg should be short with a good strong forearm, a big flat, bold knee and a short, tight, flat cannon bone. It should not be tied in below the knee nor 'back of the knee', which creates a spoon-shaped effect. The joints should be strong and clean, while the pasterns should neither be too short and upright, nor too long and sloping. The feet should be round with a strong, sound, deep frog, a

 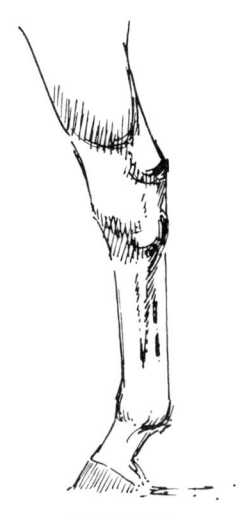 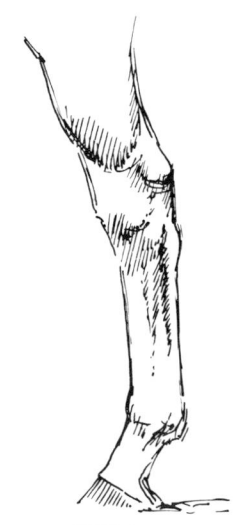

BACK AT THE KNEE   FALSE CURB   TRUE CURB

Fig 2   Conformation.

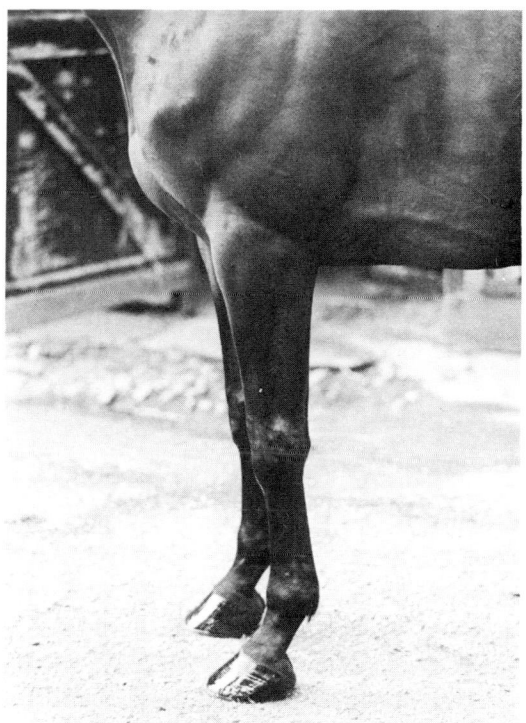

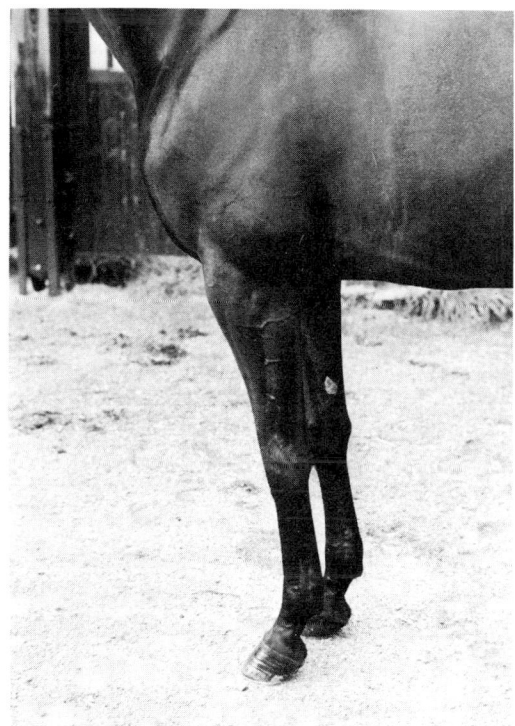

Fig 3   Forelegs and feet on a horse more suited to eventing.

Fig 4   A horse that is light of bone and tied in below the knee, with small feet.

strong sole and, above all, wide and open at the heel. The horse must in no way be flat-footed. White feet should also be avoided as they are brittle and cause clenches to become raised, resulting in loose shoes which more often than not come off.

There should be plenty of room between the horse's brisket or forelegs, allowing sufficient space for the heart. When the horse stands to be inspected he should be a leg fore square, with a leg at each corner. The back should be short, but not too short, with a good deep rib-cage from the withers down and through the back rib. The loin should be well set, deep, and have plenty of width. The tail should be well set up into the quarters of

the horse and should swing freely from side to side when he is walking or trotting. Avoid buying a horse who carries his tail to one side, as this usually suggests an injury or malformation of the quarters or back.

The horse's quarters should have a good length from hips back to tail and from hips to the point of the hocks. The horse should not be split up behind and the second thigh should be strong and have plenty of width across it, as well as being well let down into the gaskin which should be strong and sizeable. The hock itself must be wide, strong and clean, low to the ground and well set. Too straight a hind leg is a disadvantage, as is a horse

13

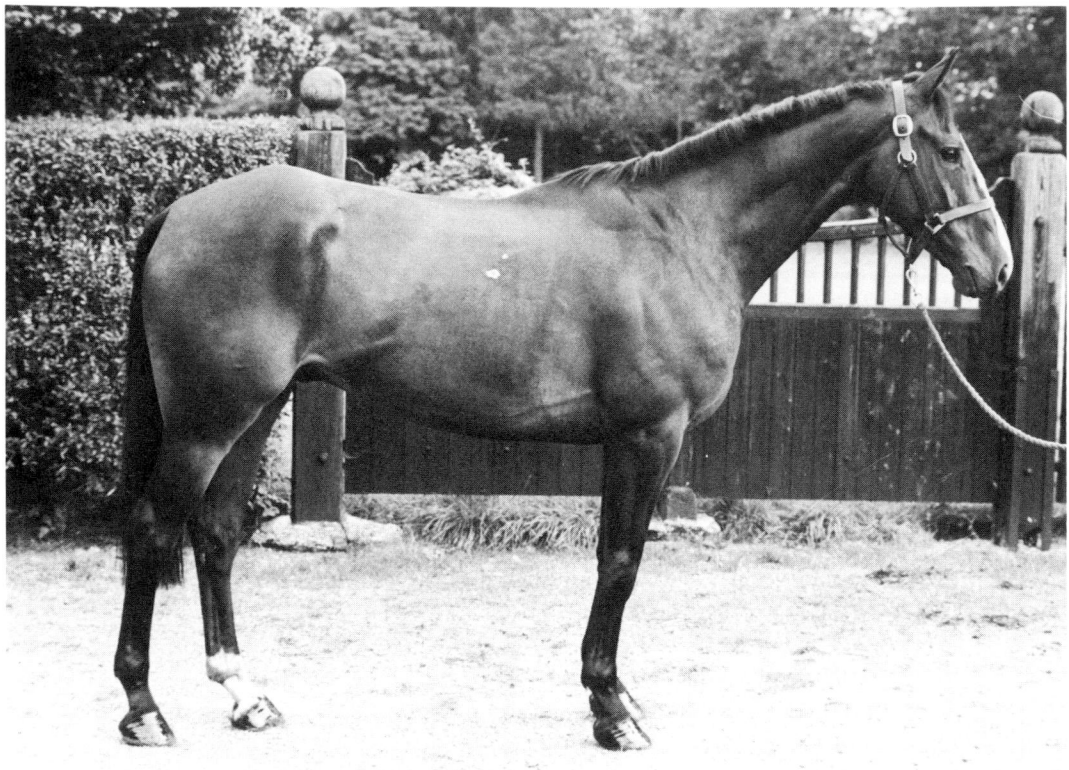

Fig 5   A suitable horse for eventing, with good conformation.

with the hocks set away from him. A useful test for a good leg is to drop a plumb-line from the point of the buttock to the point of the hock and to the back of the joint. If it touches in all three places without any daylight between each you can be fairly sure that you have found a horse with a good hind leg. Last, but by no means least, make certain the horse possesses natural balance, is a straight mover and tracts up correctly.

General Advice

In general terms there are some points of advice based on my own personal experi-

ence, that may be helpful to those seeking to purchase a likely horse for eventing. I do not like a horse with a small, mean eye or a characterless expression, nor do I like a horse with small ears close together, especially if they meet at the top. A horse with a protruding bump between the eyes is also to be avoided. All three points tend to indicate that the horse possesses a wilful streak in his temperament and, as such, will neither be kind nor generous-natured. This type of horse will probably always be looking for trouble and an easy way out.

A horse with low-set nostrils is best avoided as the air intake into the lungs when galloping can become restricted and this reduces his staying power. This can also be a problem with a horse who has no flexibility between the top of his neck and his cheek. Horses with this type of formation are often prone to making a noise.

Horses that have good, flat, hard bone are definitely preferable to those with a softer type of bone, which is prone to splint trouble. Horses back of knee are to be avoided because of the tremendous amount of stress that is imposed on the suspensory ligament at the back of the knee when galloping, which can break down. Likewise, round joints are not desirable because they are susceptible to windgalls and strain. A horse with a very short, upright pastern can be prone to jarring of the joints, while a horse with too long a pastern runs the risk of the joint nearly touching the ground when he is at speed which can cause weakness and stress in the joint.

Avoid horses with small, upright feet with no room, that are contracted at the heels, and also those with shallow feet with soft soles or with a deep-seated narrow frog. All these defects can cause lameness to varying degrees and sometimes the fault is extremely serious and incurable.

Bear in mind that a horse with a very low wither or, conversely, a very high wither, can be a problem when it comes to fitting the saddle. However, do not be put off by a horse with a roach back (a prominent rise in the back exactly behind the saddle), as they often prove to be very good jumpers. A low-set tail does not make a good picture in the dressage arena.

To be avoided at all costs are horses that have or have had 'parrot mouths', asthmatic conditions, splints, ring bones,

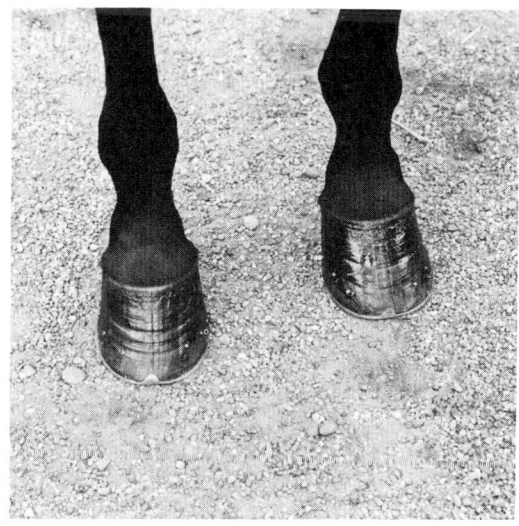

Fig 6 *Small and contracted feet not ideal for an event horse.*

sidebones, any possible sign of tendon trouble, back trouble, curbs (a bony enlargement at the back of the hock), bone or bog spavins, thoroughpins or any sign of wind defect. Any of these problems can all too easily occur anyway, so it is certainly not advisable to start out with them.

If a horse is not a straight mover, he will have problems in the dressage phase. There is always a reason for this disadvantage, which could go back to a deformity at birth, bad shoeing, or possibly a misplacement problem in the neck, shoulders, knees, joints, back, pelvis, hind quarters or hocks.

Bear in mind that a horse must be at least 15hh., five years old and have had a course of flu vaccination within the last twelve months in order to be registered for affiliated horse trials.

Finally, and very importantly, it is strongly recommended that you avoid buying a horse that is a crib biter, weaver,

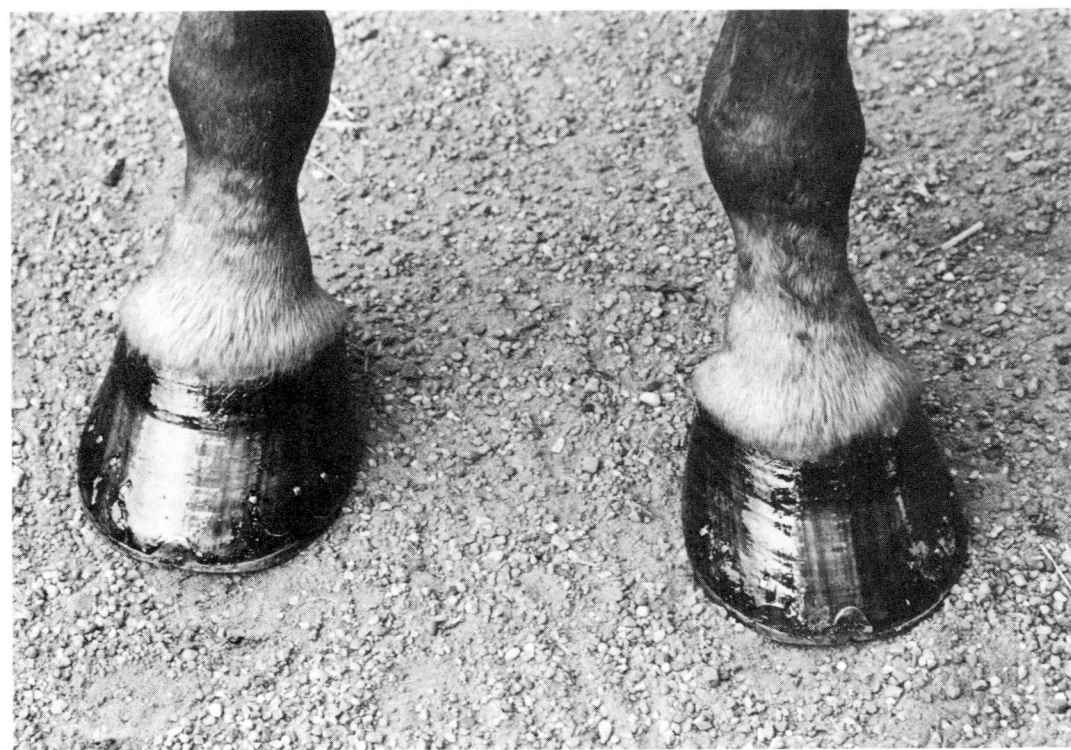

Fig 7   Good feet for an event horse.

wind sucker, box walker or bad traveller. A bad traveller is very often a man-made problem and, as such, can often be corrected with careful management.

Looking for the Horse

There are no certain places to go to find good horses. Gone are the days when you could go to Ireland, visit a remote farm and discover over a hundred horses stabled at the back. These sources have now been exposed and exploited. My own horses come to the yard from a variety of different sources; many from word of mouth, telephone calls, advertisements in local papers, computer list organisations, show jumping and horse racing yards, and trade publications. I am lucky in that people come to me and therefore I seldom need to buy from the sales or from dealers. Business in event horses is booming currently and English and Irish home-bred event horses are popular the world over. It was not by chance that almost all the horses at the 1986 World Championships in Gawler, Australia, were English or Irish bred. Indisputably, they are to eventing what the Scandinavian, German and Dutch horses are to dressage and show jumping.

The important thing about selecting and buying a horse is to have a knowledgeable person with a good eye to accompany you. Ideally, this person should be familiar with you and your capability as a rider, because age and experience are major considerations in the type of horse purchased. A novice rider, for example, would need a horse with some experience across all three phases. Finding the right horse is the key to success.

There are many sources to look into when buying horses. Certainly, a good starting out point might well be someone who has a good reputation for bringing on young horses for eventing themselves – they are likely to have put time and effort into the flat work of the horse already.

Looking at horses at racing sales can sometimes provide positive results, but you should bear in mind that those coming out of racing stables are schooled very differently to event horses and can often be highly-strung Thoroughbreds. However, there is little doubt that the Thoroughbred has the speed for galloping, a good stride for dressage and often the scope for jumping, so that if you can find a horse who also has the right temperament, there is every chance of success.

Buying horses through the newspapers and specialist publications can prove to be rewarding. However, you will be disappointed from time to time when you see the horse and he does not appear to live up to the expectations raised from reading the advertisement. Over the years I have bought and sold horses through the press, and have found that it is a good idea to telephone first for a photograph, to get a more accurate impression of the prospect prior to having to travel long distances.

Many good horses in eventing started out their lives as show jumpers. Border Raider was a Grade B horse and was sold to the States from England as a ten-year-old. Two years later the horse was second in a CCI 3-Day event in Poland, ridden by David O'Connor. Shannagh, Lucinda Green's well-known 3-Day event horse was also formerly a Grade B show jumper. The advantages that show jumpers sometimes have are that they may be older, have travelled, have miles on the clock in terms of experience, are used to competition and have the basic jumping ability. The unknown quantity is whether the horse might be too careful and unable to take the risks when jumping at speed in the cross country phase.

Whatever route you take to find a horse, it is vital to have an expert eye with you and to have the horse properly vetted. This should ensure not only that the horse is the right type of animal for the sport, is being sold on genuine grounds, has the capability to make the grade and is a sound purchase, but also, if good sound advice is taken from someone who is knowledgeable and familiar with the proposed rider, that the horse and jockey are at the right level of experience for each other. Advice here can prevent the undesirable situation of two novices together. It is also important to ensure, if the jockey is aiming for his first event having only ridden ponies, that the horse has the necessary experience, ideally in hunting, show jumping, hunter trials or even some events, if possible. On the other hand, a slightly older and more experienced event rider could buy a young horse, since he is more likely to have the knowledge and expertise needed to train the horse. If you are buying a young horse, or one with no known form, it is essential that the horse is tried in all his paces. Ideally, he should be tested by the proposed jockey in all disciplines of eventing to see how he reacts to flat work and to the jumping of different fences with a new rider. Getting a feel for the speed of the horse is important – many events are won or lost on time and it is crucial that the horse should have a good stride and gallop over the ground, not into it.

Price

The price of a horse will vary according to his record, age and experience. The only important statement that can be made on this is that the money paid has to be related to affordability, and it must be remembered that the cost of the purchase is unrelated to the ongoing running costs. As such, it is essential that the cost of tack, visits by the vet, work by the blacksmith, livery, feed, transportation and lessons are all budgeted for *before* any purchase is undertaken. A young horse at a low price may seem like a bargain at the time, but when the work, trips and different types of competition have been accounted for, even before the first event, he may not seem such good value. This is especially the case when he is compared to an older, more experienced and more expensive initial purchase, since this type of horse allows the pupil to get on and start competing at dressage, show jumping

and hunter trials almost immediately.

There are specific seasons for eventing – spring and autumn – and therefore the timing of the purchase of the horse needs to be either pre-Christmas (for the mid-March events) or around April (for the autumn events, that usually start in late July). These guidelines assume an experienced horse and a reasonable rider who will need three months working together to get fit and ready, and whose partnership will have become established by the time the season gets under way. A partnership has been established when the horse has complete confidence in the rider and vice versa, and when the horse will be prepared to jump anything, within reason, that is asked of him.

In the final analysis, everything that is done in the selection process must be geared towards bringing the partnership of horse and rider together. There are no definite theories connecting the weight and height and age of the rider to the type and size of the horse, but on average the top event horses are around 16–16.3hh. Then again, Dylan II (barely 15hh.) completed Badminton six times piloted by Polly Schwerdt. The only really important factor is to find a horse who feels right from the start. After that, hard work, preparation and talent in both will determine the ultimate success of the partnership.

2 Caring for your Horse

Once you have bought the horse, he must be looked after properly if he is going to be fit and well enough to compete. There are still many instances of horses breaking down or being in poor condition, or even being ridden in competition when either unfit or unsound. All too often the problems stem from ignorance and a failure to seek proper advice and guidance. Every horse is different and the way they should be trained and what feed should be given when, and in what quantity also varies. At the time of purchase it should be established when the horse was last wormed, given its latest vaccination and had its teeth attended to, and what the feeding schedule and content was under the previous stable management. A horse should be wormed four times a year; a routine dental inspection should be undertaken twice a year by an expert and 'wolf teeth', if they have appeared, must be removed.

When a horse has been working, part of the stable discipline should be to walk him so that he is not too hot and cools down. On a cold day his loins and kidneys must be kept covered up with a blanket or rug, and this should protect him from Azoturia. Event horses are particularly susceptible to this condition and it usually takes the form of the horse seizing up, or taking very short steps. A vet should always be called and the horse needs to be kept warm and still. Azoturia is sometimes referred to as 'Monday Morning Disease', because a horse who has had the Sunday off, has

been overfed on protein and then overworked on the Monday, is very susceptible to it. Sometimes after hard work a horse may break out in a sweat again in the stable, so care must be taken to ensure that the rugs used are always dry and warm. In the event of sweating again, change the rugs and make sure the ears and loins are dry. If necessary, walk the horse out again to relax him, and keep the movement and circulation going.

Attention to detail will safeguard a horse for a long, happy and healthy future. A few years ago, Castlewellan, my own horse, was picked for the British Team competing in the European Championship at Luhmühlen in West Germany A week before the event, I discovered, during a routine check, that he had very slight heat in his off fore. Many riders would have gone on, but I judged it would be unfair to the team and, perhaps even more importantly, unjust to the horse, to compete. It required tremendous strength of character on my part, but heeding the warning light meant that a month later Castlewellan was able to win the Working Hunter and Spillers Combined Training events at The Horse of the Year Show, and two weeks later he finished third at Boekelo 3-Day event in Holland. Interestingly, in a sport of highs and lows, this horse never had any soundness problems in his limbs throughout his career. Similarly, it is the care that I take over feeding in the yard that has enabled my horses to be admired frequently for the condition in which they are presented at an event, right from the start of the season to the very end. Good condition more often than not suggests a happy horse from a caring, concerned and knowledgeable yard.

Stable Routine

Feeding

It is not unusual to find that a horse in an environment with which he is unfamiliar will not eat properly for a while. This can often be quickly resolved by keeping the feeds small and appetising and allowing the horse time to get used to the new stable's routine. It is important to give feeds at regular times, and when eventing the horse should go on to four feeds a day with a last feed late at night. If the food is of good quality, less is required – it is critically important that a horse in training should never be over-fed. There has been much written about the feeding of horses and many people have their own theories and practices. If you are in any doubt you can always seek the opinion of a good vet. Any hay fed must only be of top quality and it is advisable to dampen and even soak the hay in clean water before feeding it to horses, as the dust contains bacteria which can cause wind problems or set off allergies.

In my yard, the first feed of the day tends to be the smallest feed as it precedes work. The lunch-time feed is slightly larger, with the tea-time feed being the main feed of the day with all the additives. To make the food enjoyable we add carrots, molasses or treacle. We control the use of hay and beet pulp, and soak the latter in water for twelve hours first. We feed boiled barley during the winter months to help keep the horse's condition and no beet pulp or boiled food is given to horses in fast work. When a horse is in training certain foods are given up so that wind and condition when working are improved.

The feeding of each horse has to be in keeping with his size, work and temperament. Some require more high protein food, and while some need a large quantity of oats, others do not. What is essential is that the feed must help the condition of the horse. To achieve this you may need to feed extra ingredients such as cod liver oil for his coat, boiled linseed (highly nutritious), or blood salts for the digestion of protein and other vitamins. There is always an element of trial and error in the search for the optimum feed. If a horse looks wrong, a blood test and consultation with the vet can establish whether the horse is anaemic. If a horse goes off his food, initially it is better to drop one or two feeds in the hope that he will find his appetite again. When a horse is fit, but not working on a particular day the lunch feed can be omitted.

It is important not to feed a horse immediately before or after work – there should be a lapse of at least an hour in each case. There must be fresh water accessible to the horse at all times, but after work the amount given should be limited to half a dozen gulps of chilled water. Only when the horse has cooled down should more water be allowed. On competition days after heavy exertion, it is advisable to give the horse a softer type of food which is more easily digestible, possibly prepared with boiled linseed or given with warm water which will make it easier for the horse to digest. A hay net can be given to a horse after he has been working or once he has recovered from the exertion of competing, but should not be given in the morning if the horse is expected to gallop across country.

Clipping

Clipping is an important task in the winter as it aids the horse to dry off properly after work. If the horse is not clipped he will remain damp and sweaty, losing condition and becoming hard to groom. After clipping it may take a few days for the natural layer of fat to form which provides protection against the cold, so care must be taken to ensure that the horse is kept warm with blankets. Clipping should not take place after the end of January as this can spoil the summer coat, although some horses will need to be trimmed or clipped throughout the year. Indeed, in extremely hot weather, at the top level of eventing one will occasionally see a horse being clipped after the dressage phase so that he stays cool for the cross country.

There are different views on the type of clip to be recommended. In general, eventers should be full clipped as they will look smarter for the spring events without trace clip lines. Whiskers can also be clipped – although they are a horse's most important organ of touch, they are far less relevant to a horse that is permanently stabled. Heels and fetlocks can be trimmed with scissors and a comb. When clipping, always cut against the coat, taking as much with one sweep as possible, and leave the difficult bits to last. Don't carry on clipping if the horse breaks out or the clippers get too hot, and don't push or force the clippers, but rather use oil and keep the clippers cool.

Daily Routine

Checking the horse's legs daily is an enforced part of the stable routine. By doing this, you can learn whether a particular horse always has a little filling in a leg after working, or whether his legs are normally absolutely clear. This is crucial, as working a horse who uncharacteristically has slight heat in a leg could create even more damage. The problem, most often caused by reaction to rough ground or concussion, is a red light warning and the horse should be laid off for a few days and given a complete rest. If you carry on working the horse hard it could result in a bad sprain and the horse being laid up for upwards of six months. Always call in a vet to ensure that no irreparable damage has been or could be done.

Another part of the daily routine is to look at the horse's coat, his eye and his deportment. If he is looking off colour he could have a chill, and working a horse in this condition could result in pneumonia. As a precaution, take his temperature, which should be 100–100.5°F (38°C), and consider whether there might have been a reaction to straw bedding (shavings may be preferable), or perhaps whether the feed needs to be changed, to provide something that is missing, or to be made more interesting. The horse's droppings should be checked daily to ensure that he is regular and that he is eating properly, as colic can easily set in. The word colic covers a multitude of symptoms which indicate abdominal pain and need to be quickly and carefully treated with veterinary consultation.

Evidence of colic is when the horse scrapes the ground, lies down and rolls, trying to kick his stomach, or sweats, or just looks distressed. The droppings will indicate whether the horse needs worming, for which there are prescribed cures. The condition of the coat, which sometimes comes up in white rings indicating dermatitis, will also be a guide to worms.

Stable Management

As stable routine is essential, so too is strict and disciplined stable management. To ignore even the smallest chore can result in a potential disaster. When a horse is tacked up for morning exercise, make sure the tack has been cleaned so that the leather is supple, that the bit is clean so that no foreign objects can rub the horse's mouth, that the correct bit is being used and that the tack fits correctly. Bear in mind that a horse should not be trained in equipment that would not be allowed in competition – so, for example, a potential Novice eventer must use only a plain bit and not a double bridle. The tack must be carefully fitted and, on a thin horse (or one losing weight), a breastplate should be added to stop the saddle slipping back.

When hacking, the horse should be fitted with kneecaps, or protective knee boots, especially where road work is involved. However, remember that these must be removed if the horse is going to gallop or jump. Check that they are well-fitting and are not rubbing, as this can cause swelling in the leg, which will look like a tendon injury. Back boots should also be worn, especially if a horse moves close behind to stop the hind joints from brushing. When schooling cross country or going through mud, over-reach boots should be worn to prevent an over-reach. Exercise bandages can be worn instead of boots. However, because horses' legs can fill after strenuous exercise, a horse can benefit from the application of stable bandages worn overnight.

To begin with, an all-purpose saddle should be used, although when the rider has more experience and is competing at higher levels, there are merits in having a special dressage saddle, which aids his position and his leg contact with the horse. A sheepskin, foam or rubber numnah should be placed under the saddle; this is important during slow work or if the rider is heavily built, in which case the horse could get a sore back from carrying the weight constantly. On a cold day, when only walking is being done, a blanket should be folded back under the saddle, keeping the horse's loins warm.

In the winter it is better to put plenty of rugs on the horse in the stable and to have good ventilation, rather than to have the stable closed up with no air. It is important that the roller which keeps the blankets on is well forward – if it slips back it becomes like a kicking strap and then the horse will thrash and kick out, pulling off the rugs, and may be in danger of causing himself an injury in the process. Even in the summer, the horse may require blankets in order to maintain a steady body temperature. Do not respond simply to the time of year, but feel the horse to make sure he is warm at all times.

The stable or loose box should be well aired and large enough for the horse to lie down in comfort and there should be plenty of clean bedding in it, made up of either straw or shavings. The sides should be banked up so that if the horse

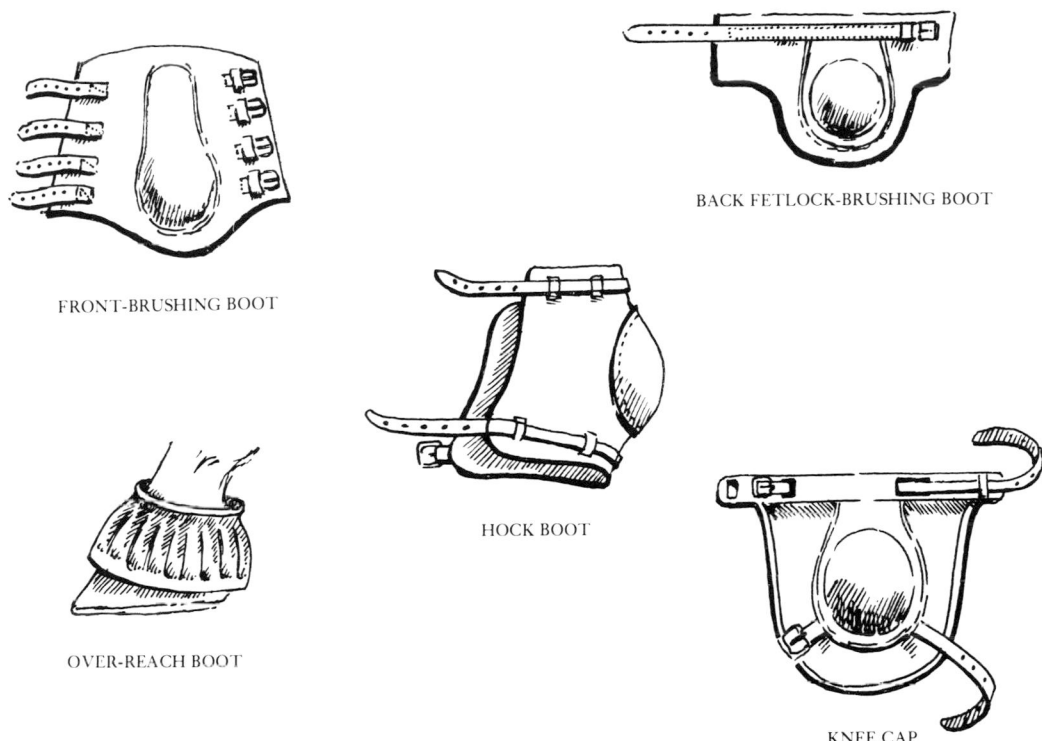

FRONT-BRUSHING BOOT

BACK FETLOCK-BRUSHING BOOT

HOCK BOOT

OVER-REACH BOOT

KNEE CAP

Fig 8   Examples of boots

rolls he won't suffer capped hocks (knocking them against the stable wall). The hay net should be securely attached, the feed trough a permanent fixture and the water bucket suspended, or in a place where it cannot be interfered with. Never leave a head collar on the horse or lying about in the stable – if he puts a foot through the collar (or, indeed, through a poorly-hung hay net that is too low), he could cause himself a serious injury. The stable must be mucked out every morning so that the horse is not on wet and dirty manure. If this is left, it is easy for him to contract thrush in the foot, a rotting disease which can lead to lameness. It is important for the stable to be comfortable, a place where the horse can relax and develop good habits, such as lying down in the afternoon.

Minor Medical Problems

Surface Injuries

Part of good stable management is knowing what to do when a horse has a minor problem that should not need to involve a vet. Any type of surface injury from rubbing, and any cuts or abrasions that occur when exercising, must be treated immediately. The injury should be washed with cold water, or water with a disinfectant in it, and then treated with wound dressing powder.

When a horse has a swelling or bruised tendon this should be hosed with cold water. A warm kaolin poultice should then be applied. This should be carried on until the swelling, inflammation or bruising has gone down, after which a cooling lotion bandage should be applied daily. A recommended dosage of the lotion should be made up with a pint of water, a gamgee soaked in it and then put on with a wet bandage, after which a cold water bandage can be applied. When an injury needs stitches, the vet should be called immediately, and while you are waiting for him, you should ascertain when the last anti-tetanus injection was administered.

Temperature

If a horse is off colour after exercise and he has a slight temperature he could be suffering from a mild form of colic. In this situation, walk the horse gently for half an hour. If still unhappy the vet should be called to check that there is nothing seriously wrong.

Foot Problems

During the winter a horse can get cracked heels or mud fever, normally the result of contact to mud. In mild cases a zinc and castor oil ointment can be applied, but in advanced cases special astringent lotions or zinc ointments may be needed, with sulphanilamide pads and bandages used to restrict movement. It is important in advanced cases, or in minor cases not responding to treatment, that veterinary help should be sought, as a course of prescribed antibiotics can help. The feed should be changed to a laxative diet and the horse must be rested.

A common foot problem that occurs all year round is a corn, which usually results in the horse going short in the front. Poor shoeing can sometimes also lead to corns in the hind feet. It will normally be caused by the pressure of the shoe in the wrong place, or by a stone working its way in between shoe and sole. In most cases rest, and the removal of the shoe with an antiseptic poultice applied is the best course of treatment. It pays to have a good farrier who, in consultation with a vet, can recommend the best shoes for each horse. Like humans, horses can have good and bad feet, and need a good blacksmith either to build them up or provide reinforcement and support. Some horses have feet that cannot stand up to the hard work and pounding across country involved in their training. This is normally due to the size and shape of the feet, or to the balance of the horse, problems which can only partially be resolved by corrective shoeing.

Sores

Saddle sores or a sore back are commonplace and can be the result of a rough or badly fitted saddle, or of a heavy rider who sits in one position all the time. The best treatment is to keep the saddle off the back and lunge the horse instead. If there is an open wound this should be treated with kaolin paste, and when it is better the scab should be hardened with salt and water or methylated spirit. It might be advisable to cut a hole in a protective foam pad, and put it under the saddle to relieve the pressure on that part of the back for a time.

Coughs and Colds

Horses will, from time to time, suffer from colds and minor coughs. These need not be serious, providing they are treated early on, with the symptoms diagnosed accurately, and the horse being rested from work and isolated from other horses in the yard. There will usually be a thin nasal discharge, a rise in temperature, and sneezing, and the coat may turn dull when the horse has a head cold. He must be kept warm in a well-ventilated stable, fed on a laxative diet and given inhalations of Friar's Balsam. The cough could be a symptom of the head cold or the result of a sore throat or something stuck in the throat. Coughs can also indicate indigestion or be due to a change in environment and feed. If it is not symptomatic of a head cold, it would be advisable to get a vet's opinion and diagnosis, as a problem such as broken wind or influenza could result in permanent respiratory trouble.

There is no substitute for an expert's opinion, and in any cases of colic, coughs and heat in the leg the veterinary surgeon should be called. There may be a simple remedy, but leaving the problem unattended could easily lead to a twisted gut, influenza or a major breakdown. While prevention may be better than cure, accurate diagnosis is always better than guesswork.

Grooming

A fundamental part of good stable management is grooming which is the key to making sure that the horse is well turned out. Ideally, the main grooming should take place after the horse has been exercised, when the skin and coat are warm and the scurf and dust have been brought to the surface.

Normally, before a horse works in the morning there will be the brush over, which removes straw from the mane and tail and stable stains from the night before. The feet are picked out at this time. The main grooming takes place later in the day, and is done once the horse has dried off. The sweat marks are removed using the dandy brush – be careful about your choice of brush as a very thin-skinned horse may need a softer body brush, especially after clipping. The key task is to brush out the dust and dirt on the coat and legs, removing mud and dirt from the heels. The body brush is then used to get any scurf out of the coat and the curry comb cleans the body brush as the grooming task is done. Finally, a cloth is used to remove surplus dust.

Looking after the horse's feet at grooming time is essential, and many stables spend too little time taking the trouble to pick out the horse's feet and treating the hooves with oil or special hoof dressing, to ensure against cracking. When the horse is in the stable a tail bandage should be used as this keeps the tail in a nice, tidy shape once it has been brushed out. The eyes and nose should be sponged out daily, while the underparts of a horse should be washed at least once a month. The horse's mane and tail should be correctly pulled by someone who is experienced at the technique – this will avoid the mane and tail becoming bushy and unruly.

However, grooming should not be done when the horses are on holiday or resting in the field. In this case, it is best to leave the mud on them, even when they come in at night, as this serves as protection from the rain and from the cold. It does the horse no harm to have a break from being groomed and from being scrubbed and rubbed down by humans. This time also serves as a welcome break for groom and rider from one daily chore.

3 The Rider's Preparation

Set Your Goals

Enjoyment and success in eventing come from the partnership of horse and rider. Owning the best event horse in the world is not enough, you have to be able to ride it. Before even considering what preparation the horse may need, the rider must be prepared. Unless the basic disciplines of riding have been taught to the pupil, both in flat work and in jumping, there is little point in turning to the sport of eventing. Once the rudiments are known, then there must be two added ingredients – courage and dedication. Courage is needed to make changes when time, or an obstacle, demand it, or to carry on when nothing seems to be going quite right. Dedication is needed to become a true eventer, since nothing is accomplished in this sport without hard work, the will to win and the determination to succeed. And even more dedication will be necessary when the tragedies and failures befall you, with regard both to your horse and to yourself. It takes a strong temperament to accept that this is a sport of highs and lows, where the most calculated preparation and plans can be undone in a single, unexpected and often unlucky moment. It is for this reason that it is so important to recognise and enjoy the high points, the successes and the achievements, because these are the true rewards of the sport. When I competed again for the first

time after my hunting accident in February 1981, it was nearly four years since my last event. Winning that Novice event after the medical experts had ruled me out because of the damage to my left leg, gave me as much pleasure as my more often recounted successes in the major events. I was back, and back as a winner.

What is certain is that each event rider has to set his own standards. Some aim just to improve, some just to get round, some merely to participate and some to win. Whatever the aim, it is the reaching of their goal as a horse and rider that is the moment of triumph. To reach this point necessitates basic riding skills, courage and dedication, and it all starts with the rider.

Fitness

The rider needs to be very fit for eventing and if the sport is only a part-time hobby it is advisable to take regular exercise in other ways. Skipping, jogging, circuit or fitness training, squash, racquet-ball and swimming are all valid ways of keeping in shape. Riding one horse a day is not enough, but if riding is all you do, then working a number of horses should provide you with the right stamina, speed of reaction and dexterity. Fitness certainly plays a major part in eventing, as you must be fit enough to walk the steeple-chase, show jumping and cross country courses, as well as strong enough to hold the horse together, and to ride with as much balance as possible. This is particularly important when you are coming to the end of a gruelling cross country course, when the ground may have been heavy, and the horse is tired and requires as much of your assistance as possible. If you are like a sack of potatoes on the horse's back at this time it could slow him right down and make his jumping more tired, resulting in serious time penalty points. Even the world's leading equestrian riders, like Lucinda Green and Virginia Leng, have been seen doing skipping exercises before major three day events where they may have two rides. Don't expect a horse to carry you – you must always be fit enough to do him justice.

Safety

The rider should always wear a safety hat or crash helmet, especially when exercising on the roads or jumping. There have been too many serious accidents which could have been avoided if the correct protective headgear had been worn. Always wear a crash helmet, even when you are just schooling over cross country fences. Furthermore, when schooling over fences you should not be on your own – if something goes wrong and you have a bad fall it could be hours before somebody finds you. It is always as well to notify people at the place where you are schooling when you arrive and when you depart.

Posture

Correct posture on a horse is essential – if the position of the rider is crooked or with a collapsed hip it is difficult for the horse to go correctly. A video camera and/or a mirror in an indoor school are the best aids, other than a trainer, for checking your position. However experienced you are, continually check that your seat is correct, that your back is straight, your head up and your legs in the right place. The rider must neither look down nor lean forward or back. Leaning forward will encourage a horse to run on, and get on its forehand. Leaning back means the rider is behind the movement of the horse and, if he is naughty, the horse may throw his head and even buck. The horse must be ridden from the rider's legs and seat, and into the hands. The legs create the impulsion, the energy and forward movement, while the hands receive it and control and distribute it, thereby influencing the horse, and gaining his trust and confidence. Too many riders try to ride with hands, failing to realise that it is not the hands that make the outline of the horse, but that this is created by seat and legs.

The hands need to be in co-ordination with the rider's legs and weight and not used in a backward movement to pull and stop the horse. Pulling a horse in the mouth is an unforgiveable sin as this will develop an insensitive mouth and can often make a horse unhappy. The hands are there to be used in different ways, according to the degree of experience of the horse and the way he is going. They must not be dead; the horse should obey them, and they should enable him to improve in the schooling and in the making of transitions. Good hands are a

Fig 9   Incorrect position with elbows out and rounded wrists.

natural gift but every rider should try to improve, and develop hands that are sympathetic, quiet and sensitive. They should not move up and down, or be too stiff and hard and they should be carried as if you were reaching out to shake a hand, with the thumb being the highest point. The fingers should be light on the reins and should not pull hard on the mouth. If a horse pulls, the rider should give rather than pull back – this means that the horse has nothing to lean on or pull against, and he will become light and

more sensitive to the hand as a result.

The arms should lie against the body, while the lower arm should form a straight line from the elbow to the horse's mouth. A common fault is where the arms are too straight, causing the horse to resist against the hands.

In order for the legs to exert the right influence they must be in the correct position. The lower leg should be just on the girth and the knee and heel pointed down with the latter in a straight line with the body. There should be no grip

Fig 10 Here, the leg is too far forwards and therefore the position is incorrect.

Fig 11 The rider is leaning forward in an incorrect position.

Fig 12   The rider is leaning too far back with collapsed hips.

with the knee – the contact with the horse should be through the calf muscles. When a horse 'comes on the bit' it means that the leg is being correctly used to engage him. The hand receives the energy and gently steers the horse, giving it a round outline. This is the correct way to ride.

Exercises for Rider's Position

An important training discipline for the inexperienced rider, taught on the lunge rein, is practising balance and posture. An experienced and responsive horse with an unflappable temperament and nice steady paces should be used – this means that the rider does not have to be thinking about controlling the horse, but is free to concentrate on the use of the leg, the position

Fig 13   *Correct dressage position, riding in a hacking jacket.*

Fig 14   *The correct hand position for a dressage seat.*

Fig 15   *A rising trot with the rider's arms too straight.*

Fig 16   *Gripping with the knee – incorrect leg position.*

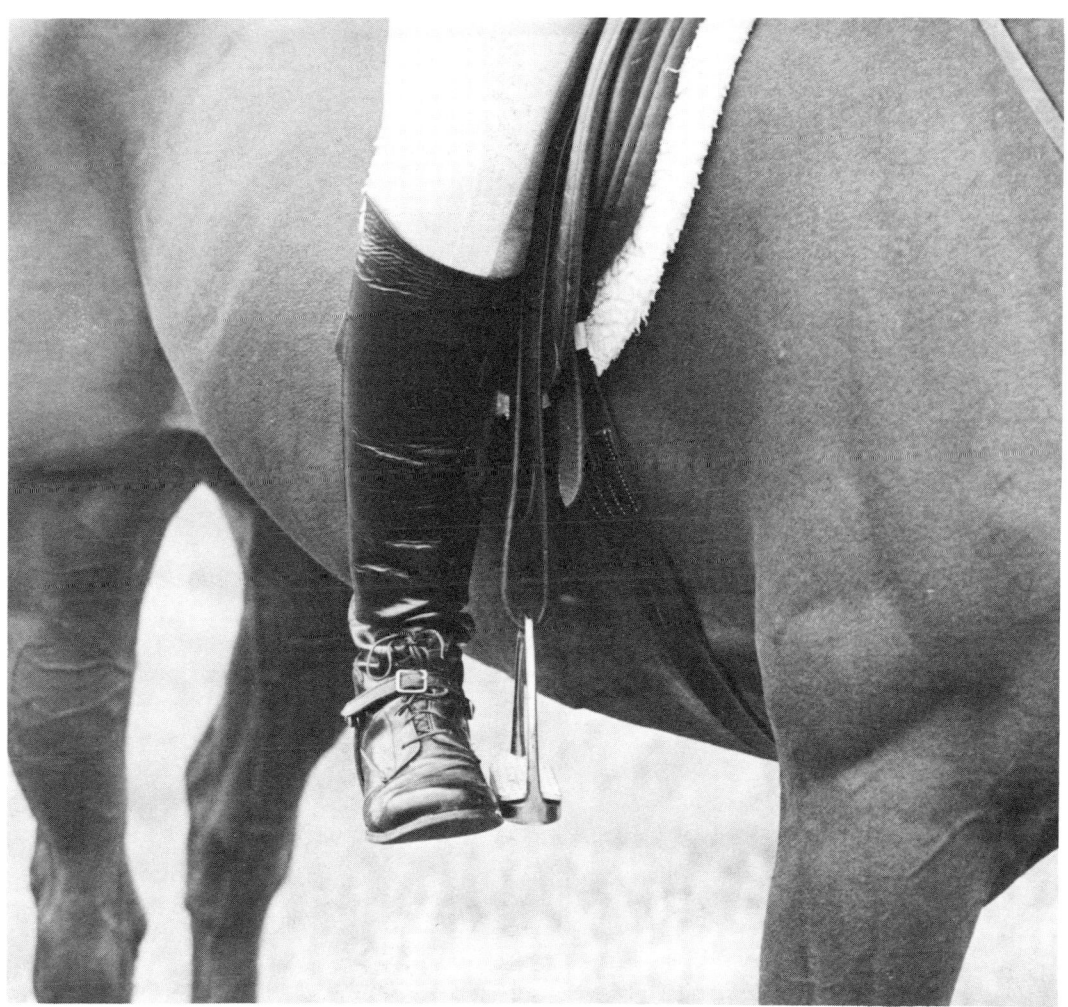

Fig 17 The correct length for dressage, showing the ball of the foot level with the base of the stirrup.

of his feet and his posture in the saddle. This exercise should be done without stirrups, enabling the rider to let himself down into the saddle, 'sitting the movement out'. Assuming the horse is calm and settled, only side reins will be necessary and the normal reins can be knotted. However, to begin with it may be sensible to allow the rider to keep the reins for confidence, and also to allow the horse time to accept the rider bouncing up and down, and teach him not to react to out-of-balance movements. The exercise should be carried out at a sedate, working trot pace and the rider will learn to absorb the rhythm of the trot, rather than being bounced up and down. Often riders get tense and grip with their knees, but they should relax and let the leg hang down long and sit to the horse.

There are other exercises that can be carried out on the lunge rein to practise balance, such as trying to get the hand to touch the opposite foot or knee, leaning across the horse. Another is learning to bring the leg up and away from the horse so as to let the seat down into the saddle and not rely on grip for position. Arm and back exercises, such as keeping your arms in front of you and holding your head up are all valuable ways of working on posture. More experienced riders will practise with different lengths of stirrup; this will aid balance and strengthen their seat for cross country.

It is important for the person lunging to give the appropriate corrective instructions, aids and commands, so that the rider is helped. An experienced instructor holding the lunge rein can transmit the control to a good rider who, just by using his legs, can give the horse the instruction on pace and movement from the saddle. Even if there is no one to help with lunging, the discipline and practice of riding without stirrups is invaluable. Over time, it will help the dressage and the confidence of the rider as his movement on board will be more in rhythm with the horse, his seat will be deeper, he will sit to movement. He will gain the confidence to lengthen the stirrups to the correct length, causing him to sit well into the saddle.

The Rider's Temperament

A good rider will never lose his patience or his temper with the horse, but will be resolute and patient, especially in schooling. There are moments when a horse may need to be punished, but there must also be a reward when he gets it right. A horse is like a child and you must be fair, treating him with a firm hand but always being sympathetic and understanding, so that a feeling of trust and confidence emerges as he grows up. No horse should be allowed to get away with doing things wrong as this leads to bad habits which are hard to cure. However, at the same time, it is important not to demoralise a horse as this can make him resistant and it will be difficult to enthuse him and get him to work properly. Teaching the horse obedience to instruction will enable you to get him to do what you want, when you want it.

While this book is not about learning how to ride it is important to remember that, however good you may think you are as a rider, you can always learn more. Riding is an art and a skill and perfection is achieved by few. Each horse and each event poses a fresh set of problems to overcome. Youth has courage and bravado combined with raw natural ability. In time, experience and training will enable the rider to get the best out of a horse and to consolidate his strength, while pacing a competition correctly to the advantage of both. Always be ready to learn more, whether it is about posture, doing ground work, show jumping technique or cross country approach. Accept criticism and be self-critical at all times. It is no longer sufficient to be able to go across country at speed; nowadays, being able to pace the horse, and having the precision of a good show jumper and the discipline of a top dressage rider are also essential. Competitions are won and lost across all three elements, and your horse can do none of them without you.

Use of the Whip

The rider's use of the whip bears careful examination as it is all too often misused or not properly understood. At home, on a young horse, a whip should always be carried in case there is a need for correction – a distraction on the road, for example, might well cause the horse to resist. Here the whip is used as a means of teaching a horse obedience. When a horse is simply lazy a long dressage whip can help to get him to engage more from behind, or merely to wake up and appreciate that this is time to work. It is not advisable to use a long dressage whip on the roads, but preferable to use a normal whip.

When doing show jumping, or cross country, a whip should be carried, if only to keep the horse's concentration, correct him or simply to encourage him through a difficult obstacle. It is also important to teach the horse that it is not acceptable for the brakes to go on unexpectedly or for him to run out at an obstacle.

In competition it is advisable to ride in with a whip even before dressage, only releasing it before going into the arena. In show jumping and cross country carry the whip with you. In the cross country phase there will be occasions when the horse is lacking in impulsion coming into a spread fence; taking the whip out also gives the rider added strength in the leg that can get the horse out of trouble. Sometimes a young horse will need encouragement before going into water and here the rider should take the reins in one hand and the whip should be used gently once behind the leg on the flanks.

4 Training the Inexperienced Horse

The way a horse has been broken in can determine his nature and attitude for the rest of his life. The ideal programme is gradual, letting the horse have plenty of time to get adjusted, first to having tack on, and then to having something on his back. It is good if this can be done in an indoor arena with a lunging rein and for a while the horse should be given the chance to gain confidence, and to learn to trust the handler. Encouragement and a reassuring hand throughout are really important as not surprisingly, most horses get scared by what they do not know and cannot see but can feel. It is important to take time over the breaking in of the horse to allow him to get used to each stage.

Start by lunging the horse freely and only gradually introduce different items. The roller should be tried first, then the saddle without leathers and irons, then with the leathers and finally with the stirrup irons. Only when the horse has got used to the saddle and the girth, and is not resisting or frightened, should the rider be introduced. To begin with, the rider should lie across the saddle to teach the horse to accept this sudden extra weight on his back. Eventually he will be able to sit in the saddle for short periods, but without using either stirrups or reins. (The horse should still have the confidence of the lunge rein throughout these progressive steps.) Gradually the horse will accept the saddle, the rider and, eventually, the bit.

Fig 18   Feeling the horse's tendons before work.

Flat Work

Flat work is the basis behind all riding and concentrating on this will provide a balanced horse who uses the right muscles to go forward, being propelled from behind. It is essential that the rider does not pull the head and neck in, but rather develops the outline by pushing from behind, letting the strength come

Fig 19   Allowing the horse to stretch while working.

from the horse's hind legs. This will enable the horse to go forward to the hand. In the early stages, both horse and rider will benefit from expert help and advice on the correct method of schooling and how to strengthen the horse's muscles; this will also ensure that the rider is using the aids correctly and taking the desired approach.

Hacking

Hacking is very important for a young horse and to begin with, if it is possible, he should be taken out with an older horse who is well accustomed to traffic and being out on the roads. This should help the young horse to get used to traffic and the roads and prevent him from being frightened by all the sights and strange elements – when he eventually goes out

alone, he will be less likely to shy at these or refuse to pass them. It is vital to hack over various terrains, experiencing traffic, and getting the horse familiarised with different settings such as woods and open country, as well as undulating countryside and roads. These all help to widen the horse's experience of life, while introducing him to many of the situations that may be encountered later in competition. When hacking, it is important for the horse to be on the bit and to be ridden properly and not allowed to amble. Hacking out with an indifferent rider can teach a horse extremely bad habits. If he is allowed to amble, his muscles will not be used correctly and he will not be conditioning himself to move in the right way and to form the right shape. This is where hill work can help as it will develop the jumping muscles, teach the horse balance, get the hind legs underneath the horse, as well as making him think where to put his feet. Hills also help a horse's stamina, strengthening the heart and lungs through greater exertion. All these exercises should be done at a controlled walking or trotting pace.

The Arena

In order to school a horse properly there should be an arena, which can be erected in a flat field or in an indoor school. It is an advantage to have this marked out, correct in both shape and size. The arena used for the Novice test should be 40m in length and 20m in width, while the more advanced tests are executed in an arena of 60m × 20m. While it is not essential for it to be exactly this size, it is beneficial to have some idea of what the arena will be like in competition.

Set the arena out with markers. To begin with, when working the horse in the arena get him to bend correctly in both directions and to learn leg obedience. This means teaching the horse to go away from the inside leg, which can be done by leg yielding. The horse must learn to be straight, adapting to the track he traces whether this track is straight or curved. To aid the horse in the very early stages, it may be easier to work in a larger area so that the movements can come naturally without the horse immediately being constrained by a confined area.

Fig 20   This is a good outline for a Novice horse in a working walk – the rider is in a good position and there is sympathetic contact.

Fig 21   A working walk in an incorrect position – the horse is above the bit.

Fig 22   Working walk – the contact is not positive enough and the outline needs to be rounder.

Fig 23   A trot with the horse's neck incorrect. It is too high at
the poll and the outline is not right.

Fig 24   Showing a better outline, but the rider's shoulders are
a little rounded.

It is particularly important to ride correct circles and school movements when working a horse. While an indoor school with sand for wet and cold weather is a distinct advantage, it is not a limitation if only a field is available (except in times of heavy snow). Indeed, so many of the events in the early part of the year in Britain encounter snow, wind and rain, with dressage rings sometimes situated on the side of a hill, it is actually beneficial to have ridden the horse outdoors. All my horses are ridden indoors and outdoors all the year round except when there is snow, ice or hail. Riding them in the different weather conditions and in varying parts of a field helps to familiarise them with different locations and ground that is less than perfect. This helps them to become better balanced, while preparing them for the inclement conditions that can be expected at many events.

Riders who have to school outside in all weathers will have the advantage over riders who have schooled most of the time indoors. This difference is seen most often at the early spring events when you can expect to encounter bad weather. Horses that are not used to working in the wind or a heavy downpour can become unsettled and excited by these conditions.

Schooling

Before schooling a horse you need to know the basic dressage movements, so that you can be sure that the movements, figures and circles you practise are those that will be required in competition. As a dressage judge I see so many marks dropped by the horse and rider clearly having ridden incorrect school figures.

By learning the correct basic way to ride circles and turns with accuracy you will avoid throwing away marks unnecessarily in competition. However, it is essential never to rush the horse, but to give him time and to exercise patience.

In the early days the horse should be hacked out daily for about an hour. Some days it may be better to lunge the horse and then hack or school him for half an hour to three quarters of an hour. Importantly, vary the work and do not expect the horse to do the same thing day in and day out as this will become boring for both of you. When riding the young horse try something new a few times one day, do something different (or more familiar) the following day and only go back to the new movement the day after. Finish on a good note even if the work time has been short on that particular day. Always encourage the horse, pat and reward him when an effort has been made or when he has got it right, and be tolerant – the horse has to work it out just as much as the rider. Achieving smooth transitions between movements comes with practice and it is important not to ride the horse in such a way that anticipation replaces response. By varying the exercises this potential problem should be averted.

As the flat work becomes stronger and more controlled it will become worthwhile to take the horse to small unaffiliated dressage events, where competition can be experienced, yet the stakes and demands will not be too high. It will help the horse to have an outing with other horses and to encounter a marked-up arena with a central line. Ideally, a number of tests should be completed in the day – at least two or three, and even as many as four – and you should not be

Fig 25 A rising trot – the head is tipping and there is a little mouth resistance.

surprised to find your horse getting flustered and excited in the first test. As such, it is good to go back into the arena again so that he learns to be obedient and calm. Over two or three tests the horse should become more relaxed and ready to accept the situation, the surroundings and the presence of other horses. From the rider's standpoint, it is good to get used to riding a number of tests under the pressure of competition. This helps the rider to get accustomed to the horse and his mannerisms in competition, and to learn how to get the best out of the horse even under difficult conditions or when the horse is being uncooperative. This is all part of 'getting miles on the clock', and experience is one thing that cannot be bought. The really good dressage riders gain every mark going by being careful, accurate and precise and even when their horse is not going superbly they never throw marks away. This can make the difference between being placed and finishing nowhere.

Jumping

When it comes to jumping, always make sure you are wearing a crash helmet with a chin strap. A young horse should be schooled over small fences, starting with a loose school with no attachments or rider, or on the lunge. Place a pole 2½yds (2.30m) in front of the jump to indicate the correct distance for take-off. Lunging the horse without a rider allows him to learn to jump without the extra weight, thus encouraging him to think only of the fence and not of the rider on top. When the rider is introduced, use a placing pole then a cross rail. Only slowly build up to bigger fences and only gradually widen the spreads. Introduce the horse, both indoors and outdoors, to the types of fence that can be encountered in a show jumping class, so that they become familiar. This means rustics, brightly-coloured poles, planks, bricks, gates, stiles, combinations, spreads and uprights will all need to be included.

Exercises

To help the horse's suppleness, and to build up his trust and confidence in the rider, it is a good idea to do gymnastic exercises with poles and cavallettis. Three or four poles should be laid approximately 1yd (1m) apart (for a 16hh. horse) – this distance will vary depending on the size and, more importantly, the stride of the horse. The horse should move through the line at a working rising trot, maintaining the same speed and tempo. When the balance has been established, the cavalletti, or a small jump 14in (35cm) high, can be added about 2½yds (2.30m) on from the last pole.

Once this has been successfully negotiated, additional cavallettis or small jumps can be added at intervals, allowing the horse a stride in canter between each. The distance should be 3–3½yds (2.75–3.20m) between the first cavalletti and the second, so that a bounce is created. This would be for approaching in trot. When in canter, increase to 4yds (3.65m).

Fig 26   Approach with a trotting pole in front as a guide to take-off.

Fig 27 Jumping the first part of the double – an upright.

Fig 28 Landing and moving on to the next part.

Fig 29   Using a pole as a guide to the second part of the double.

Fig 30   Taking off at second element of the double – a parallel.

Fig 31 Jumping the second part of the double accurately.

This type of exercise will improve the balance, co-ordination, agility and confidence of both horse and rider. Eventually a jump can be added at the end of the line, and hopefully by then the relaxed and still position, adopted in the early phase of the exercise, will be continued through, and there will be no sudden exaggerated forward movement of the rider's body.

A further development of the exercise is to raise the poles slightly off the ground, which will improve and develop the horse's rhythm and cadence. This type of work calms a horse down in jumping, aiding obedience and making the horse think where he is putting his feet. Rhythm is all-important so that the horse learns not to rush into, run on or dive at obstacles. Because a young horse lacks concentration at times, rather like a

young child, you need to be patient and repeat exercises quite often. In order to gain the horse's confidence, in the early days the exercises and jumps should be situated along a wall of the indoor school or a fence in a field. Lunge lessons over raised poles will also help the horse's movement while making him use his shoulders more.

When it comes to jumping, expert and specialist trainers can be of invaluable assistance, as they understand how to make the horse clever and improve his technique. It is always possible to help the horse with a long stride to shorten it, and the horse with a short stride to try to open up and jump on a longer stride.

As with dressage, it is useful to take the young horse to unaffiliated shows, indoors and outdoors, where the experience of being around other horses and jumping a variety of obstacles at a controlled speed is good learning. In the early days stick to novice and newcomer competitions, and do not move on to Foxhunters or larger courses until the horse has shown real confidence and ability over the smaller obstacles. Do not rush a horse and be careful not to race the young horse against the clock in jump offs. The danger is that, by asking the horse serious questions at speed, you can undermine his training and technique and this can lead to him getting over-excited and jumping flat.

Preparation for Cross Country

Taking the horse out and jumping small ditches is essential, even early in his career, but to begin with this should be done with an older more experienced horse giving the lead example. The important thing to be wary of in doing this is frightening the young horse by asking it to jump something too big too early on. The experienced lead horse will show the young one how to jump a small ditch, and this should give him confidence so that he is not caught out. After following the experienced horse, go back and jump it alone with the young horse. If he refuses to jump it, then punish him, but if he does jump, you should reward him. The horse must learn to jump everything small with confidence and then the bigger obstacles will be jumped without hesitation. You will find many times, when riding a young horse in a Novice event cross country, that if he encounters something that looks different and difficult he will go on because he trusts you. This faith will have been built up over the period of schooling and training at home.

Once the horse is jumping ditches then it is as well to find or erect other makeshift cross country obstacles; alternatively, you could take the horse for a school over some easy practice fences at a Pre-Novice or Novice event course. It is vital for the horse to encounter different types of fences – hedges, logs, drops, water, ditches and coffins. A horse that has hunted will have learned to cope with any type of going and different weather conditions, which will prove to be a distinct advantage when encountering wet muddy conditions at any event.

Taking the horse hunting is good for both horse and rider as it makes them bolder, as well as reactive and ready to take things on, especially if there is a ditch in front and a drop on the landing side. The rider needs to be quick to respond to unexpected situations. Hunting is also good for horses because they gain the experience of jumping a variety of obstacles and fences, of being with other horses and of moving over different terrains. Another reason why I like to take my young horses out cubbing or hunting is because it toughens them up. A young horse that has been doing mainly dressage and show jumping may become a little precious and 'flashy', with a tendency to 'spook' at the unknown. Taking them hunting widens their experience and gets them used to ploughed fields, muddy terrain and wet and windy conditions. All this will pay dividends when it comes to eventing, especially in the spring season. It is also good for the rider to go hunting on different horses without having to compete, as this teaches him to adapt his riding style to suit each particular horse. I have been lucky enough to be on the borders of some of the best hunting country, with the Belvoir, Cottesmore and Quorn all within easy distance, and nearly all my young horses (including my dressage horses) hunt in the autumn and up to Christmas.

However, before going hunting you must make certain that the groundwork has been done by jumping small fences cleanly and accurately and learning about water by following another horse through a puddle, a stream or even a pond or lake. Always start by taking each new experience slowly and, in the case of water, you must proceed by walking into it, ensuring there is not a boggy or false bottom. The horse must never be allowed to become frightened, least of all when young, as a bad memory can last forever. That is why you must start small and only slowly build up, so that confidence grows all the time.

Maintaining the Horse's Interest

Riding club events, hunter trials and unaffiliated small cross country events are all good experience prior to going on to the bigger competitions and the more small events that can be taken in the better. They bring variety to the horse's training so that there is interest and enthusiasm in his work, with new challenges to keep the keenness and contentment. Always try to find new places to go, new fences to jump and new exercises to learn, even when bringing on the young horse at home. Turning a horse out in the field every day for an hour, when the weather permits, helps him to become settled and prevents stable boredom. To begin with, turn the young horse out with a calm and docile horse that is older and unlikely to kick. If the young horse seems to settle easily then it is fine for him to be turned out on his own. During the cold spells, turn the horse out with a New Zealand rug which has leg straps.

Always ride the inexperienced horse with sympathetic handling and remember that, while there must be obedience and respect, the horse must always be allowed to keep his own character. There must be punishment for disobedience but a reward for good work. All my career I have found that the horses with character and a touch of cheekiness, who are harder to ride to and train, are the horses that will give and achieve the most in competition. As a rule, the docile, tranquil, easy horse lacks sparkle and often braveness, excitement and keenness for the sport. For this reason you should not try to rule over a horse and take his character away, but rather you should work *with* him, most especially in the early formative years of the partnership.

5   The Equipment and its Use

It is important early on in the preparation for eventing to establish what tack is permissible for the different disciplines. This will become your guide as to what equipment to use on a horse when schooling and training at home. This chapter will try to cover the basics and explain what needs to be taken to an event and why.

Tack

Dressage

It is important to read the rules book carefully as only certain items of tack are allowed for a Novice dressage test. A simple snaffle bridle and bit are mandatory. There is a wide variety of snaffles and it is a question of experimenting to discover the type that your horse goes best in. Each will have a different effect on the horse, and certainly the horse will have a distinct preference for one over others. It is essential to ascertain this as it can make a difference of several marks on competition day. The most common types of snaffle to try out are a German (thick) snaffle, a French snaffle with a double joint, a cheek snaffle with side pieces, and an eggbutt snaffle.

The noseband for dressage should be a plain cavesson, drop, flash or grackle. Great care must be taken to ensure that it is fitted correctly so that it cannot interfere with the horse's breathing. It should be tight enough to stop the horse from opening his mouth wide or being able to cross his jaw. A breastplate is permitted, and should be used if there is any danger of the saddle slipping back. This normally happens on a very thin horse, when a horse is losing weight, or when the horse has 'run up light' and condition and weight have been lost.

The reins for dressage should be thin and ideally should be in plain leather or plaited leather, although rubber is acceptable. If rubber reins are used the rein stops should be taken off, not only because they look untidy, but also because they can emphasise any unevenness in the contact when the horse's head moves.

In the rules book you will find a comprehensive list of tack that is not permissible. This includes an eggbutt snaffle, any form of martingale or draw reins. In the dressage arena itself, no boots or bandages of any description may be worn, nor may a whip be carried.

The rider's equipment for competition is also subject to change and therefore the competitor must consult the rules book annually. If you are in any doubt, contact the authorities for clarification, guidance and direction. Basically, the competitor's attire should be the hunting dress of breeches (white or beige), black boots (brown are permissible if worn with a tweed jacket at Novice level) and a white stock, although, at Novice level, a coloured stock or tie is permitted. The

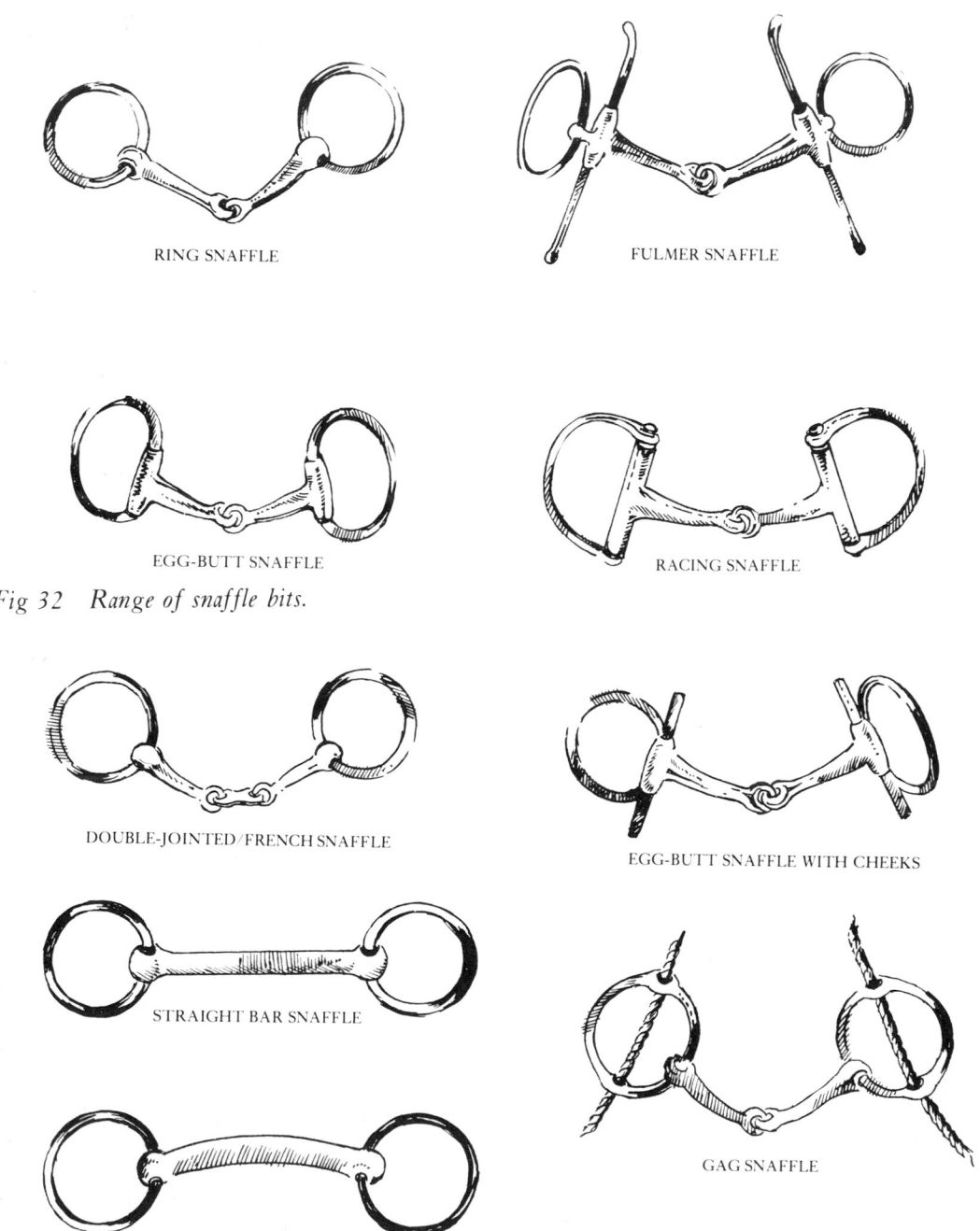

RING SNAFFLE

FULMER SNAFFLE

EGG-BUTT SNAFFLE

RACING SNAFFLE

Fig 32   *Range of snaffle bits.*

DOUBLE-JOINTED/FRENCH SNAFFLE

EGG-BUTT SNAFFLE WITH CHEEKS

STRAIGHT BAR SNAFFLE

GAG SNAFFLE

HALF MOON SNAFFLE

Fig 33   *Range of snaffle bits.*

coloured stock or tie may only be worn if a black or navy jacket is not being worn. A black or navy jacket should be worn with a black or blue hard hat of the same colour. Spurs are not compulsory, except in FEI and Advanced tests, but they can be worn at any level as long as they are blunt. Gloves are compulsory in the dressge phase at Intermediate level and above and must be light coloured (a ruling introduced in Britain in 1987).

The saddle should be of an English type and dressage, jumping and all purpose saddles arc all permitted. If it is affordable, it is preferable for the competitor to have both a dressage and a jumping saddle. The dressage saddle will help the rider to sit in a better position with his weight placed correctly, so that the horse's balance is improved. However, for the person starting out with unknown potential, an all-purpose saddle is probably more practical. A sheepskin or foam numnah should be worn under the saddle. This is particularly important when riding a Thoroughbred horse as they tend to have thinner skin and need to be given adequate protection so that they do not drop their backs. Some numnahs have a thicker pad under the saddle and are thinner where the legs go. This is ideal as it does not prevent the leg from getting close to the horse, while still giving the horse the protection he needs. For competition riding pads can be put into a zip cover which makes them look more elegant.

Fig 34   A correctly fitting dressage saddle.

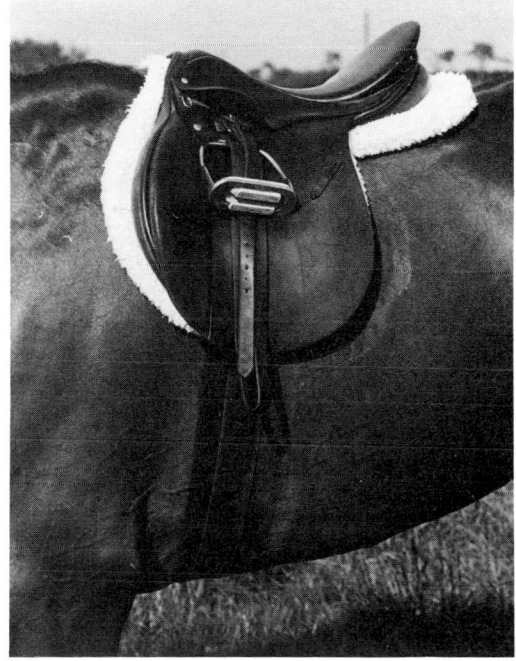

Fig 35   A correctly fitting jumping or cross country saddle.

Show Jumping and Cross Country

In the show jumping and cross country phases it is compulsory for the rider to wear a crash helmet. This may or may not have a velvet cover to make it look more like a riding cap for show jumping. The rest of the rider's dress for show jumping must be the same as for dressage and the competitor's number allocated for the day must be worn in all phases. Spurs may be worn but, again, they should be blunt and therefore must never have pointed ends with spikes. A whip is permissible but must not exceed 30in (76cm). For cross country the rider may wear a coloured sweater of his choice but breeches and boots must be the same as for dressage and show jumping.

For cross country rubber reins are often preferred as they can provide a better grip. The running martingale can be used at horse trials and the stirrup leathers should be in rawhide as these tend to be stronger – in fact, they are virtually unbreakable. For cross country ensure that the running martingale is not tight because this can catch the horse off balance when landing, especially if he is dropping into water. Riders have their own preference over saddles. Some like the flatter seat so that they can slip back at the drop fences, while others feel more secure with a deeper seat. I like to have a suede knee roll as it provides greater contact with the saddle at the leg and knee.

The stirrup irons should be made from good steel and when riding cross country you should use feet grips because the soles of your boots can often become wet and muddy, and without grips your feet may fail to stay in the stirrups. The irons

should be big enough so that, should there be a fall, the foot cannot get trapped – this could result in a broken ankle, foot or leg or the rider could be dragged along. It is for this same reason that I never allow any of my riders to ride a horse when wearing wellington boots.

While the girth for dressage should be in leather, because it looks smarter, the webbing girth is preferable for cross country. Always use two girth straps – if one should snap the saddle will be kept in place and not fall off the horse, or slip round his stomach.

Boots on the horse are important as protection but it is a matter of choice as to which should be used. I tend to use open-

Fig 36 Show jumping and over-reach boot.

fronted boots for the show jumping phase so that the horse will feel it if he hits an obstacle, and will then tend to respect his fences better. If the horse is too protected and hits a pole he won't feel it and may not have sufficient respect for the rest of the obstacles. I usually use over-reach boots for both show jumping and cross country as a precaution to prevent the horse from over-reaching and sustaining an injury that can take a long time to heal. For the cross country I put either bandages or boots on front and hind legs, but it is important that bandages are put on correctly by somebody who is experienced. Make sure they are securely fastened with tape and, ideally, stitched. Otherwise, not only will they look bad, but they can also cause damage by applying the wrong pressure or by coming undone and trailing, sometimes with disastrous consequences. Boots are a good safeguard (on both front legs and hind legs) when doing cross country, especially if the horse raps or knocks its legs against the solid obstacles. They must be well fitting and care must be taken to ensure that they don't rub the horse. I have seen many horses contract an infection where they have been rubbed by the boot, and what was seemingly a small problem has

Fig 37   *The correct tack and dress for show jumping, including open-fronted boots in front.*

Fig 38   The horse and his rider ready for the cross country phase – note the surcingle and breast plate.

resulted in a swollen and tender leg, bad enough to cause lameness. This should be overcome by having boots with sheepskin lining or using 'Fibre-g' leg protectors. There is still the danger of dirt or sand getting in between the boot and the leg which can cause sufficient friction to create a problem. Ensure that the legwear cannot impede the movement of the fetlock joint. This can be avoided by making the bottom strap looser than the other straps.

Maintenance

The tack should always be carefully checked to ensure that the stitching is intact and that there are no weaknesses in the leather. Even with regular oiling and the application of saddle soap they will inevitably become rotten and worn out over time. Snapping leather can happen to the best of us and at the most unfortunate times. A few years ago at Badminton a senior competitor in contention lost any chance he had when a rein broke after the sixth fence. The bridle also needs to be strong. As far as the bit is concerned, it is for the rider to determine what the horse will go best in. Snaffles, Pelhams, double bridles and gag snaffles are all permitted.

What to Carry with You

Maintenance of both your tack and your clothing is, therefore, important. It will be extremely costly to replace and will quickly go rotten or break if it is not looked after carefully and conscientiously. Saddle soap, sponges and a metal polisher should accompany you wherever you go with the horse. The metal polisher should be used on the stirrup irons, the bit and head collar buckles.

First Aid

When travelling it is a good idea to have a basic first aid box. This should contain a thermometer so that if the horse is off colour his temperature can be checked. There should be a disinfectant so that you can attend to a wound immediately – if this runs out you can clean the wound with cotton wool soaked in salt water. An antiseptic spray, wound dressing spray and powder, plus cooling lotion, should all be contained in the travelling medical chest. Bandages, kaolin poultices, gamgee, animal lintex and antiseptic cream should be stocked. A bandage may be necessary if you need a tourniquet for a particularly bad wound. Also, if the horse has arrived at an event in travelling boots then it is advisable to bandage him on the return journey, prevention being better than cure. A poultice should be used if the horse has hit a knee and you should apply plenty of padding all round the joint so that the bandage doesn't cut in, making the skin sore. If the horse returns slightly jarred (often the result of concussion from hard ground), apply the cooling lotion and bandage the legs.

Always carry some colic drink which can be administered if there is any suspicion of the horse going down with this condition. However, if there is the slightest suspicion, and the horse-box has not yet left the competition event, then get the horse seen by the vet on duty. Plenty of towels should also be carried so that on a wet day the horse can be properly dried off before being rugged up and put back on the box.

Grooming Equipment

A hammer and pincers should be carried with the grooming equipment, so that if a nail comes loose on a shoe it can either be hammered down or, alternatively, the nail, and in some cases the shoe itself, can be removed. It is as well also to carry the right length nails for the horse in case one is lost from the shoe during competition. A hoof pick should always be included so that the feet can be properly cleaned out. A sharp pointed nail is also necessary so that the stud holes can be picked out quickly and easily. While the blacksmith on the ground does have nails, my horse-box always carries a spare set of shoes.

In the grooming kit there should be elastic bands and a needle and thread for plaiting, as well as the right brushes and equipment to groom the horse properly at the event, both before competing in the dressage phase (when squares can be put on the horse's hind quarters), and at the end of competition. Nowadays squares or diamonds can be most easily made by a plastic, shaped pattern, although they can be created by carefully-designed brushing strokes, or by using a comb. For the end of the day you will need good sponges, a sweat scraper and a bucket so that the horse can be washed down after jumping cross country. Take plenty of water. You should also take hoof oil that can be applied before the horse goes into the dressage arena to improve his overall appearance.

Rugs and Numnahs

When travelling with the horse you should always carry sufficient rugs and blankets. The horse should have a smart day rug to travel in, under which may be worn blankets and/or a cotton sheet, depending on the weather and temperature. After the competition, or heavy work, a cotton sweat sheet should be put on to help the horse dry off. This, or a thermal rug made of 'Thermatex' through which his skin can breathe, should be put on whenever a horse is hot and sweating. This will keep him dry, while letting heat and perspiration come through. A waterproof rug may also be needed if the horse is being walked before being loaded up and it happens to be raining. The loins and back of the horse must be kept dry at all times when he is not actually competing. Always take extra blankets in case it is very wet or the temperature drops suddenly. When the horse travels, the blankets should be kept in place with a roller, which must have a foam pad under it to prevent the horse from getting a sore back or wither. If there is any danger of this moving back towards the stifle (normally a problem on a thin horse), use a breastplate to keep it in place. Tail bandages and even, in some cases, a tail guard should be put on to stop the horse rubbing his tail. It is advisable for a horse to travel in knee boots and, if he is known to kick, hock boots might be needed as well.

Always travel with a couple of numnahs – because they absorb sweat from the horse these should be washed frequently. However, before washing in detergent, check that the horse is not allergic to the soap product. This can occur with a horse with sensitive skin and may result in sores or skin infections, leading to a sore back – this will necessitate resting the horse until his back and skin are right again.

Other Essentials

In the summer months carry a fly repellant. This will need to be applied just prior to the dressage test as marks will be deducted for any shaking of the horse's head or swishing of his tail – these movements will be interpreted as resistance rather than irritation from flies. Be careful with any chemicals such as fly sprays or coolants, as they can cause blisters on some horses. When applying the fly repellant it is best to use a cloth, rubbing it down the neck, front and head of the horse, being careful not to get it into his eyes.

When stabling away always take a feed manger, a bucket for water and mucking out equipment. It is as well always to have these things in the box but otherwise, draw up a list and keep it posted in the front of the cab to check against every trip. Do not forget to add to the list the flu vaccination certificate as most events and stabling establishments demand these. Without the certificate you may not be granted stabling, especially if it is a racecourse, and this might result in your not being allowed to compete.

It is good advice to carry spares of important equipment to fall back on. Most riders have encountered the situation where the horse has chewed through a rein or the headpiece of the bridle, where the stirrup leathers have looked faulty along the stitching or where the head collar has snapped or weakened.

Don't forget that even when the horse is travelling he needs feeding. If it is a long excursion he should be given a hay net, and even on a shorter trip a hay net should be taken for the return journey. If a lunch feed is part of his routine don't expect the horse to go without food all day as missed feeds on a tired stomach can result in colic. Be aware that if a horse has been used to shavings and, when away, suddenly discovers a straw bed, there is a good chance that the straw will be devoured. This will neither be healthy nor aid his chances of performing well in the competition. Allow for this eventuality and ensure that a muzzle is taken. Always make sure there is water for the horse to drink (although this should be controlled after exertion and should not be given until the horse has cooled down).

Clothing

From the rider's point of view, make certain that there is a spare pair of breeches in case it is raining or you fall into the water, or you split your first pair. Also, take a second pair of gloves as riding with wet gloves on a cold, damp day is very unpleasant. It is also as well to have a spare stock. I always wear one under my sweater as it provides protection for the neck. The history of the stock originates from the golden days of hunting when it was introduced to give support to the neck in a fall, perhaps even preventing it from being broken. Most riders in Britain wear a stock, while Americans tend to wear open-neck shirts. This is probably due to the fact that there is little hunting in the States and therefore few

American riders are aware of this British tradition, and perhaps are unfamiliar with the functional purpose and benefit of the stock. For additional safety I always wear a back protector for cross country, roads and tracks and steeplechase. This has not yet been made compulsory in eventing, but is now mandatory for jockeys racing under rules. The back protector will help you if you land awkwardly or if the horse kicks out in falling.

Shoeing

Shoeing is an important part of looking after the horse and ensuring that the right equipment is being worn. Shoeing should be taken very seriously and only carried out by experts. Take consultation from a vet in the first instance and then regularly from the blacksmith. The whole well-being of the horse's feet and horn can depend on the care taken over shoeing and even the balance and movement of the horse can be altered by the shoeing technique employed.

In principle a horse should be shod regularly, at least once a month. During the early part of the season, when slow work and hacking is being carried out on roads, it may be necessary to have him shod every three weeks. Leaving a horse's shoes on for more than five weeks can be dangerous, since the feet can overgrow them and this can result in corns. If a horse is closely coupled at the back and brushes against himself in movement, it might be necessary to have feather-edged shoes (secured on the inside) or three quarter shoes, to prevent the horse suffering bruising or even abrasions. Some horses have the habit of

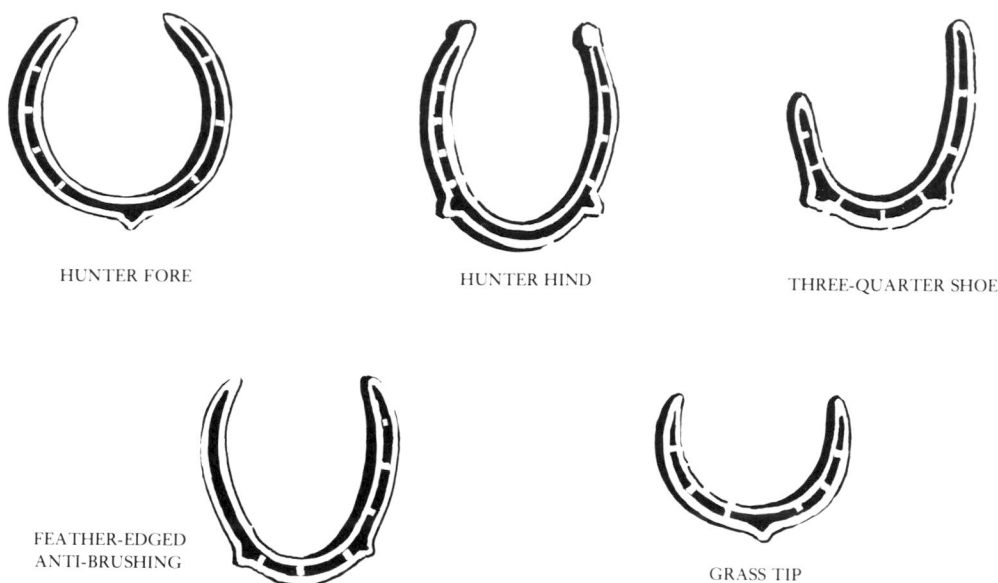

HUNTER FORE   HUNTER HIND   THREE-QUARTER SHOE

FEATHER-EDGED
ANTI-BRUSHING   GRASS TIP

Fig 39 Normal shoes for competing horses (not showing stud threads).

wearing their shoes out quickly by drag-ging their toes. To compensate for this the horse should be shod with a steel strip through the toe, thereby increasing the life of the shoe.

At the start of the season, when the horse is doing normal flat work, the shoes will not need to have stud holes. Once the build-up to competition starts in earnest, then it will be important to have stud holes incorporated, both for cross country schooling and for outdoor show jumping. In order to prevent the stud holes from becoming blocked up it is the usual practice for riders to use cotton wool plugs or road studs. These can simply be taken out or unscrewed easily and replaced with other studs suitable for show jumping, cross country, dressage, or different ground conditions. A span-ner should be carried to ensure that the screws are properly fixed in.

It is as well to note that, in the same way that racing drivers change tyres according to ground surface or weather conditions, so the rider can make his stud selection. If the ground is hard, or the going is reasonable, small studs on the outside should be sufficient. Certainly, this is the way my horses are equipped for dressage, unless the conditions are atro-cious. If the ground is muddy or heavy then a larger stud, or even a square stud that will cut into the ground, may be necessary. Sometimes the surface will be greasy while the ground itself is hard (usually after a rainfall) and in this instance a small stud with a slight point might be advisable both in front and behind.

Fig 40   Hind studs being put in for cross country.

Always be extremely careful if studs have been fitted and try to use fewer rather than more. If the rider falls off considerable damage can be caused by the studs, should the horse tread on him. Despite this, it is reasonable to expect a horse to go far better with studs in, as they will often give him a feeling of security and more grip when turning or on corners.

Equipment must always be kept tidy and clean, must be well maintained and must be in plentiful supply. This way, your response in emergencies can be prompt and effective. If, for example, there is an injury to horse or rider this means that the curing process can be started immediately. An unfortunate incident with your tack can be avoided by checking every item carefully, looking after it and having replacements at hand. With regard to feed, or the maintenance of the horse, you should have every eventuality covered and should be confident of being totally self-reliant. From the rider's standpoint it is important to be ready for a sudden change in the weather, and to have the right clothes to keep warm and dry. The golden rule is to come prepared as this will avoid any last-minute panics and enable you to concentrate on the job in hand, without unnecessary worries and pressures that are not related to the competition itself.

6 The Key to a Good Dressage Test

Riding well in the dressage phase is absolutely essential – when the going is good and the cross country course is riding well, an event competition (particularly a one day), can be determined by this first phase. A poor dressage score will invariably put you out of the hunt for a good placing at the end of the event. Event riders in Britain are often criticised by the dressage purists on five counts:

1. Failure to get the horse to use his back and hocks correctly during the test.
2. The rider being round-shouldered, with the head tilting or dropping, because of the seat not being deep and secure enough.
3. The knees being higher than the toes preventing the rider from sitting deeply enough into the saddle.
4. Over-use of the spurs and leg movements that are too obvious; rare use of the spurs and discreet leg movements are much preferred.
5. The hands being either held down and unsympathetic of the horse, or too active and pulling, not letting the horse come to the hand.

These shortcomings can all be corrected by working at them, being aware of your failings and being prepared to accept criticism and make the necessary alignments. Remember that for dressage tests at any level there are the collective marks, given at the discretion of the judge, based on the overall impression of the way the horse performed his natural paces, of his obedience and of the position and ability of the rider. These marks can be crucial at the end of the day.

Preparation

It is essential to work the horse in according to how his temperament is best suited. The important thing is to have the horse in the right frame of mind, and in a co-operative mood for the short duration of the dressage test itself. So many horses have been overridden before the test. Hours of flat work go into training the young horse before this day and it would be sad to throw it all away in this manner before the competition itself. A tired or resistant horse will start to lose his concentration. A tense horse may just need a lot of relaxing work to settle him. However, remember that something that has not been taught time and again at home cannot be learnt by the horse on the day.

If the horse is really relaxed it should work through his back making it supple. It should also work from behind, helping his balance, and preventing him from going on the forehand and thus having to rely on the hands for balance. The horse should not be over-bent but should have a good outline with the nose in front of the vertical and the head not high at the poll – a common fault among many event

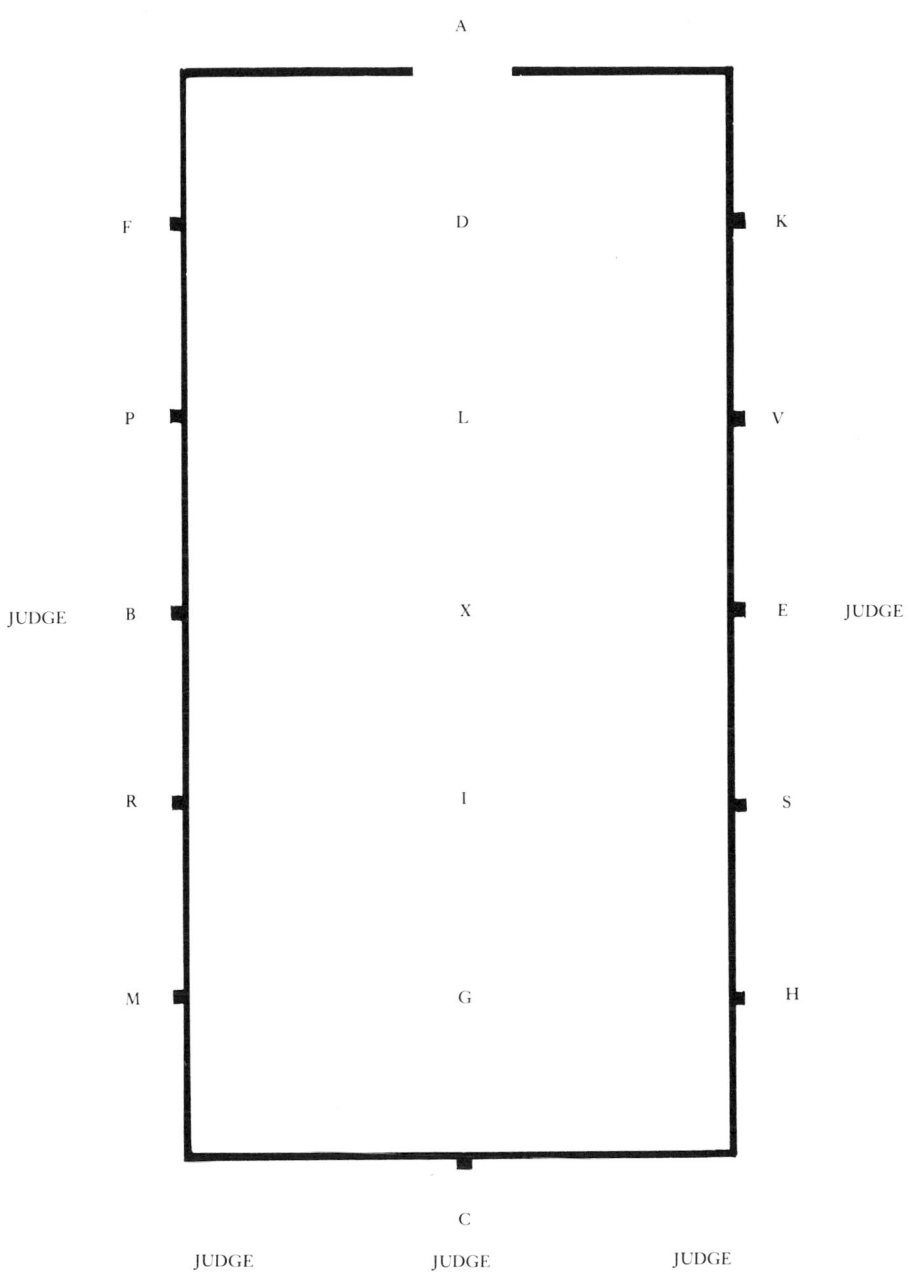

Fig 41   International dressage arena.

horses, who may be being asked too much too soon. A number of riders with young horses push them on too quickly through the Novice stage to Intermediate, with the result that they are doing Advanced tests without having been sufficiently schooled and balanced earlier. The horse must learn to accept the rider's hand and come to the hand and not come from it, which is shown by the horse's head being high and 'peacocky'.

There are no golden rules for preparing a horse at the competition for the dressage test. Some of my horses have needed as much as an hour's work on the lunge, followed by an hour's schooling, in order to be settled and disciplined before the test. This might entail working the horse to achieve concentration and suppleness with various dressage exercises. Other horses will need just thirty minutes from being saddled up to the time of the test itself. My top horse in 1986, High There, was exemplary in this way. I can also recall (in the same year that I won Burghley) arriving late at Stokenchurch with a Novice horse and the Advanced horse, Don Camillo. Both horses in the outside area were very fresh, bucking and leaping about but when they came to do their tests, they gave their all, accepting the rider's instruction, and both finished up with the best score in their section. Another horse that day had been ridden constantly for two hours by a well known horseman, and was naughty in the arena simply because he had become demoralised and was taking the opportunity in the test to 'get his own back'. It all comes down to finding the key to getting the best out of each horse on the day.

It is the rider's task to find out how to relax the horse and to get him in the right frame of mind to be able to accept the rider's demand for the test required. The key is to prepare the horse in a relaxed way, getting any freshness, stiffness or tension out by working on a long rein (making him relax the back so that all the muscles are free), before moving on to more concentrated work. Each horse will require a different plan of preparation. I have seen horses being worked in the outside arena who seem to have the paces and the test down to a fine art and look very good, but once ridden in the arena they decide that they have had enough and give nothing. Others will do nothing except amble round the outside arena and yet, when they do their test, they respond precisely to their rider's instructions. Never will the trust and confidence in a partnership be more evident than in the dressage phase, as it is here that one is truly exposed and little can be disguised.

When you are at the competition, bear in mind the fact that the judge is aware of your horse trotting round, so avoid doing any of the movements included in the test at which the horse is not particularly good. For instance, if the horse does not have a good extension, avoid doing extended trots, but rather work at a pace that shows the horse off at his best. Also try to enter the arena on the horse's best rein. If the horse is tense or slightly excitable on the day don't stop him; keep him going so that he is having to think and work while moving forward. This is far more likely to relax the horse than halting and making him impatient.

The rider must also be calm and relaxed, as a nervous rider can transmit his worries to the horse and make him tense and excitable. Even if you feel butterflies try to give an impression of calm control to the horse, as this can instil confidence and trust in him.

The Test

When the bell, whistle, hooter or horn goes try not to keep the judges waiting, as this will only be irritating to them, as usually they are facing a long day. When a rider goes completely around the arena again rather than stopping, changing direction and entering as soon as possible after the signal has been given, it merely extends their judging time. When riding the test look as though you are enjoying it, and when halting at the end smile at the judges – it might even earn you an extra point for a positive attitude. When you leave the arena ensure you leave at walking pace on a long rein. Do not cut the corners, but come round the side of the arena and leave it calmly and under control. Never punish the horse as soon as you get outside, because if the judge looks up a mark could be deducted under the heading of overall impression. Pat the horse and look pleased, so that the judge perceives you as a sporting competitor who will not set a bad example to other competitors by taking it out on the horse. Sadly, even good riders have gained bad reputations with judges and fellow competitors alike for being hard and even cruel on their horses. This can only be detrimental to the sport and results in an unhappy horse, never a pleasant sight to see. The situation is quite unnecessary as the fault can often be attributed to poor preparation over too short a period.

Remember that the attending Steward and the judges have the final say. It is

Fig 42   Entering the arena.

Fig 43   Leaving the arena on a long rein. This is the correct position for a long rein walk.

possible that a horse that is unlevel or lame may have marks deducted by the dressage judge and might not even be allowed to continue in the competition that day. This decision must be accepted by the competitor.

Make sure that you know the test. Learn it and, ideally, try and ride it on other horses you may have at home, and not merely on the horse that will have to do it on the day. The test at a Horse Trial has to be ridden from memory, with commanders or readers only being permitted at certain dressage competitions. Do not continually practise the test on the competing horse as it will start to anticipate the movements, usually with disastrous consequences. Practise some of the movements on a different horse and meanwhile ride the test through in your

mind. There is no excuse for throwing away marks by going wrong in the test. However, should you go wrong, listen to the judge's correction, try to relax, go back to the previous movement and start to think ahead again. Two marks lost may not be a disaster, providing the recovery is prompt and controlled. Further involvement from the judge during a test will happen if, in his opinion, your horse is lame, and in this case he will stop the test. Whatever you may feel you must not argue; accept their observation and retire gracefully.

Mistakes

When the rider does make an error by departing from the direction or pace laid down for the test, his attention should be

Fig 44   The correct salute at the end of the dressage test, with the horse attentive.

drawn to it immediately and the precise error pointed out. Errors can happen to anyone but when the first costs two marks, the second four, the third eight and the fourth elimination, it is essential to be prepared and to have learnt the right test carefully. There are other common errors that can be made which will not be notified immediately to the rider but which will still result in a loss of marks. Riders sometimes fail to take both reins in one hand and salute correctly. This is done by dropping the hand and saluting with it, in the case of a woman, or removing the hat and bowing the head in the case of the man (unless he is wearing a

chin strap in which case his salute will be the same as the woman's). Deductions could also be due to the rider using his voice to instruct the horse, commencing a movement from the wrong marker or making the required transition late or early.

Common Problems

It is an invaluable aid to have your test put on video and played back in the evening, ideally with a trainer, so that a check can be made on both the rider's position and the accuracy of the test, making it a learning exercise. A common

Fig 45   At the end of the dressage test – patting the horse after the salute.

fault with the less experienced rider is a tendency to rush through the test, making it difficult to have proper poise and balance, and cutting corners, along with a number of other minor inaccuracies, each of which will lose marks. When there is a halt at a marker the rider's shoulder should be parallel with that marker. Again where the transition to trot is called for, many riders only start to execute it at the point itself and therefore end up being up to four strides late. If the horse is given a warning such as a half halt several strides before the point where the transition should be made, it is likely to be more accurate. The more experienced riders rarely throw away marks, and this enables them to come out with a good score even though the horse may not have been going particularly well. The reverse will often happen to the inexperienced rider, whose horse may be going very well, but who will throw away a mark per movement for inaccuracy. The greatest discipline is always to be thinking ahead to the next movement and this should assist in the preparation. Thinking ahead also helps to keep you in a positive frame of mind when perhaps the current movement isn't going as well as you would like.

Another common failing often seen

in competition is the younger and less experienced rider being afraid to correct a mistake. If the horse strikes off incorrectly into canter, it is essential to correct it or there will be a great loss of marks for continuing the canter on the wrong leg. You will lose far fewer marks if the correction is made well, rather than letting the error become compounded. A video can pick up all these points and ensure that the rider learns from these early experiences for the next time. It will also demonstrate whether the horse was bent correctly, whether his pace was right and whether the rider's instruction was clear. Be self-analytical and critical as this will improve both accuracy and performance, as well as serve as a learning aid. Even now I try to get random tests put on video in order to study my position and the way the horse is going, and assess any corrective measures that should be taken, thus getting the maximum out of a test. I will also go through the tapes with my pupils and get them to make criticisms. This makes them more aware of how to pick up points and where not to lose marks unnecessarily.

Training

Having said all this, effective riding in competitions can only be achieved through extensive preparation and hard work at home. Only in this way can the horse be brought to his first event, ready and knowing what to do in the dressage test. Captain Eddy Goldman, who trained Sheila Willcox, Lorna Clarke, Angela Tucker and myself, among many others, instilled in us that there are three crucial stages in developing and training the horse for dressage, which are all closely interrelated: *free forward movement* which entails developing the propelling power of the hocks so that the horse learns to push himself forward from behind; the *carrying capacity of the hocks* where the horse learns to place more weight on the hind legs and the balance adjusts with the forehand becoming more raised; this will lead to the horse developing *self-carriage*. This will mean that the horse will carry himself in a well-balanced way above the ground.

When starting out the young horse is in the first stage and will be lower and longer in outline. This will improve and he will start to develop into the second stage as the schooling progresses and the transitions and way of going improve the outline and balance. This work is far more valid than simply hunting, or allowing the horse to be ridden by an indifferent everyday rider who merely wants to hack out. The horse cannot be ridden correctly on the bit until his balance and movement are right, and this can take varying lengths of time. Gradually, though, the strength will develop from the activity of the hind leg, and the hocks will become more firmly engaged and will be brought well under the horse, with the weight coming back onto them. The schooling must be undertaken daily, so that the horse develops his muscles and concentration and comes into a round outline with the hocks engaged.

It is important that the inexperienced rider should not pull or force up the young horse's head by leaning back in the saddle and pulling on the reins. This will cause irritation and resistance that can lead to a horse rearing dangerously. It is imperative for the rider to go with the movement of the horse. This will stop any resistance and encourage the horse eventually to accept the bit and the instructions. Another common mistake made by riders expecting too much too soon is putting the draw reins on and pulling in the nose, head and neck before the horse has achieved a good stride pattern. The result is that his stride shortens immediately and the stride pattern is broken and can become choppy – this can even cause the horse to become 'bridle lame', with one stride being longer than another. Take time and let the horse gradually learn to accept more, but never destroy his natural paces – only work at improving them.

Lateral Work

When working with the horse it is imperative that the rider should be disciplined enough to ride on both diagonals in rising trot so that the horse is even on both sides. Many horses have a diagonal they favour and the tendency is for riders to sit on the one being favoured, rather than encouraging the horse to accept the rider's weight on both. Some horses will

be found to be stiffer on one side than the other and in this case you will need to do lateral work, teaching the horse to go away from the leg and then going on to shoulder in movements, making the horse more supple and better balanced. The horse must learn to become leg obedient so that he goes away from the leg and does not fall in on a circle or a turn. To begin with, try this in an indoor school or down the side of a hedgerow and ask the horse to bring his quarters off the track with his head facing the wall. Eventually the horse should learn leg obedience. This fault of falling in is a common problem with older horses, and show horses who have not been schooled properly.

The horse should always be straight. A horse is said to be straight when his axis is adapted to the track which he is tracing, whether this track is straight or curved. An indication of this is whether the rider can always see the inside eye – the horse's neck should not be bent too much, while the bend should be even throughout the body.

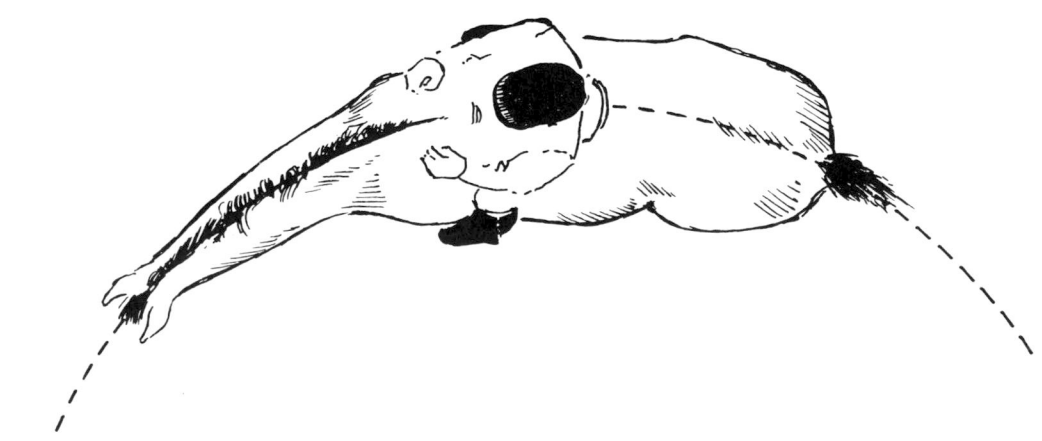

Fig 46   Correct bend, turning on a circle.

The Half Halt

One of the first movements a rider must learn is the *half halt*. This is the warning to the horse that should be used before a transition, a turn, or a change in pace. This does not only apply to dressage but is an aid that is used throughout the horse's training, and often as an indication of a change in instruction, twenty strides before a cross country fence, or a few strides before reaching a show jump. The half halt is executed by closing the legs on the girth, closing the hands momentarily and by sitting up. This helps bring the horse's hind legs more underneath him, while the forehand is slightly lightened and elevated and the quarters lowered with the balance moving back onto them. The horse is immediately more attentive and ready and able to go into the next movement. This will only be effective if the horse is straight.

While the horse is being trained it is important that his mouth should remain sensitive and responsive. It can quickly become dead as a result of pulling or of hard and unsympathetic hands in the rider. Many highly-strung Thoroughbred racehorses have hard mouths, because they are continually being restrained and pulled in the mouth by stable lads and jockeys alike. If there is resistance in the mouth or the horse is shaking or tipping his head this could either be a reaction to harsh handling, or a demonstration that he is unhappy about something. Quite often the problem in the mouth results from a problem behind the saddle – if the horse is stiff in one hock this could result in the mouth being insensitive on that side. It is for this reason that the horse is educated to go forward to the hand, where the contact should be light, the rein becoming a living, vibrant instrument.

Transitions

To do dressage effectively the transitions between different movements and paces must be smooth and natural. Again it is a question of thinking ahead. Whether the transitions are upwards or downwards they must always be executed going forward and not back, and this means that the horse should never be pulled in the mouth. Using your voice in the early stages of teaching a horse can help to get the movements fixed in his mind, and can act as reassurance when he might be tense, confused or forward-bound. As the horse becomes accustomed to the riding instruction then the voice should be reduced in volume, eventually disappearing altogether. This is important as the event test has to be carried out in complete silence. To ask the horse to go forward in the transition the rider's legs vibrate slightly and the horse's hind legs should come under. The hands become relaxed to allow the horse to go on, but if the hand is too hard the horse will throw his head up. In the downward transition the rider closes the leg and the hand, the horse meets the closed hand and then the downward transition will come through.

The basic transitions from walk to trot, and trot back to walk should be practised often – they help the horse's balance and they must be good before one can progress to the transitions from trot to canter and canter back to trot. Ensure that the exercise is repeated often and with plenty of change of direction, encouraging the horse to bend correctly and evenly on both reins.

Fig 47   The halt – this is square, but the horse is above the bit.

Halt

The halt is an important movement and it is a good exercise to practise turning down the centre line and halting precisely where you would have to in the test. Repeat this several times until the halt is square with the hind legs under and not left out behind. When practising, always maintain the halt for longer than will be required in the test so that the horse gets used to standing still and doesn't get the habit of anticipating the move off after just a few seconds.

Schooling

When the horse's basic flat work is sufficiently advanced and he is moving forwards properly balanced, then you can teach him to lengthen his trot. This requires a considerable amount of work and should be started by decreasing the speed of the trot, which not only creates more energy to do the lengthening, but also prevents the horse running on to its forehand in the movement. It is much better to have a few good lengthened strides rather than carrying out a whole diagonal with the horse running on and clearly unbalanced. Again, the horse must be straight – if he is bent too much

Fig 48   The halt – this is not square, and the rider is not taking enough contact. The reins should be taut.

one way he will be inclined to break into canter (the instruction for lengthening may easily be confused with that for striking off to canter). To achieve the lengthened strides the horse must be balanced and very even on both hands; the contact must be very steady, enabling the horse to go to the hand and push from behind. You must determine what you ask from the horse in his lengthening according to the state of the ground (deep, flat or firm). Assess the conditions carefully and if the ground is deep or sloping away you must not ask for too much, otherwise the horse will break into canter, or run on to his forehand and become unbalanced and out of control.

In schooling a horse, considerable time and attention should be given to decreasing and increasing the pace, coming from working trot back to a slower trot for a few strides and then back up to working trot, and even forwards into a medium trot once the horse is ready for this movement. The same should be done in canter – from working canter up to medium and back again. The technique for increasing and decreasing pace is similar to that employed in the transitions. These exercises help the horse's balance and improve the way the horse is going. Similarly, the decrease and increase of the circle (from a 20m one to a 10m one, and then increasing it again),

Fig 49   This is not a good halt, being hollow, with the legs out behind. The rider's lower leg is also too far forward.

will help in getting the horse to bend more correctly, and encouraging more engagement from the hind legs, and this will result in an easier and more pleasant ride. Be careful to keep the hands level throughout because if one hand is carried higher than the other, it can cause the horse to start to tip his head. Tipping the head is a common reason for riders losing marks in a test and it is often caused by horses falling in. The correction is to make the horse go away from the rider's leg – either by leg yielding or by doing shoulder in. Both exercises will help the horse to take more contact from the outside rein, which in turn should reduce any tipping of the head.

When working the horse in the arena start by getting the circle correct and executing it at walk, trot and canter. You will find it helpful to mark the tangents of a circle on a wall or on the ground. Riding circles is a continuous turning discipline over 20m, where the horse must be on a continuous curve and not ridden into the corners of the arena. Practice is essential so that eventually you know automatically what shape and size the circle is. Make certain that the turns are begun early enough and that control is kept with the outside hind leg, in order to prevent the horse swinging his quarters. It should be almost as though a magnet is drawing the horse and rider towards the centre line

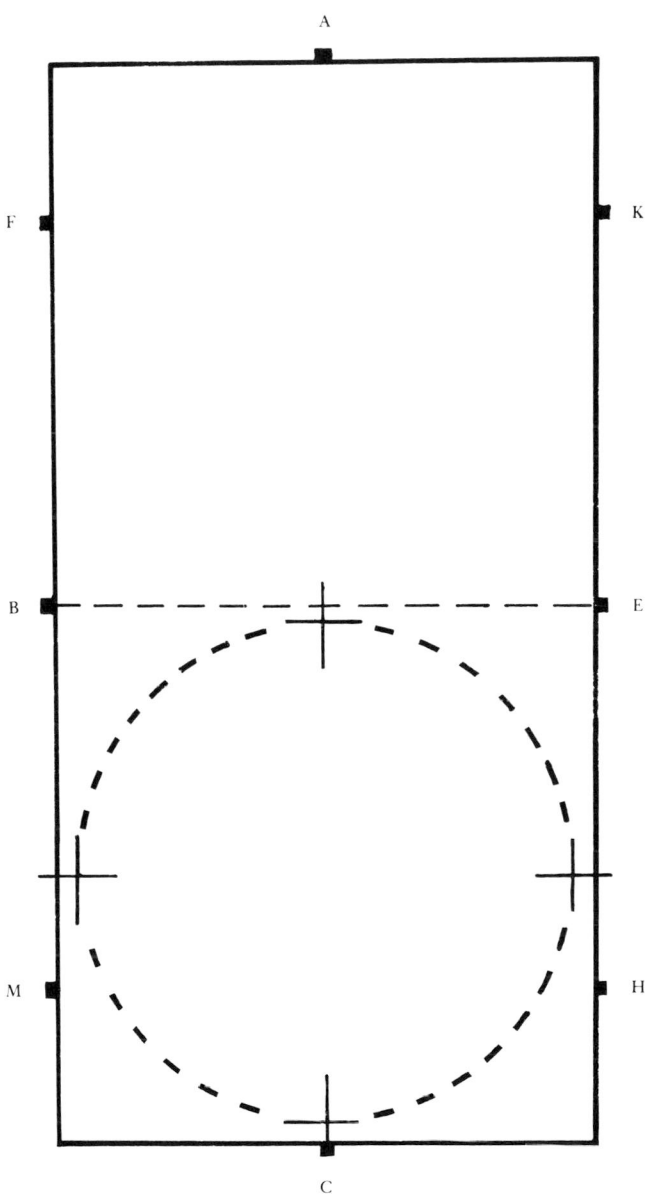

Fig 50   A twenty-metre circle showing four tangents.

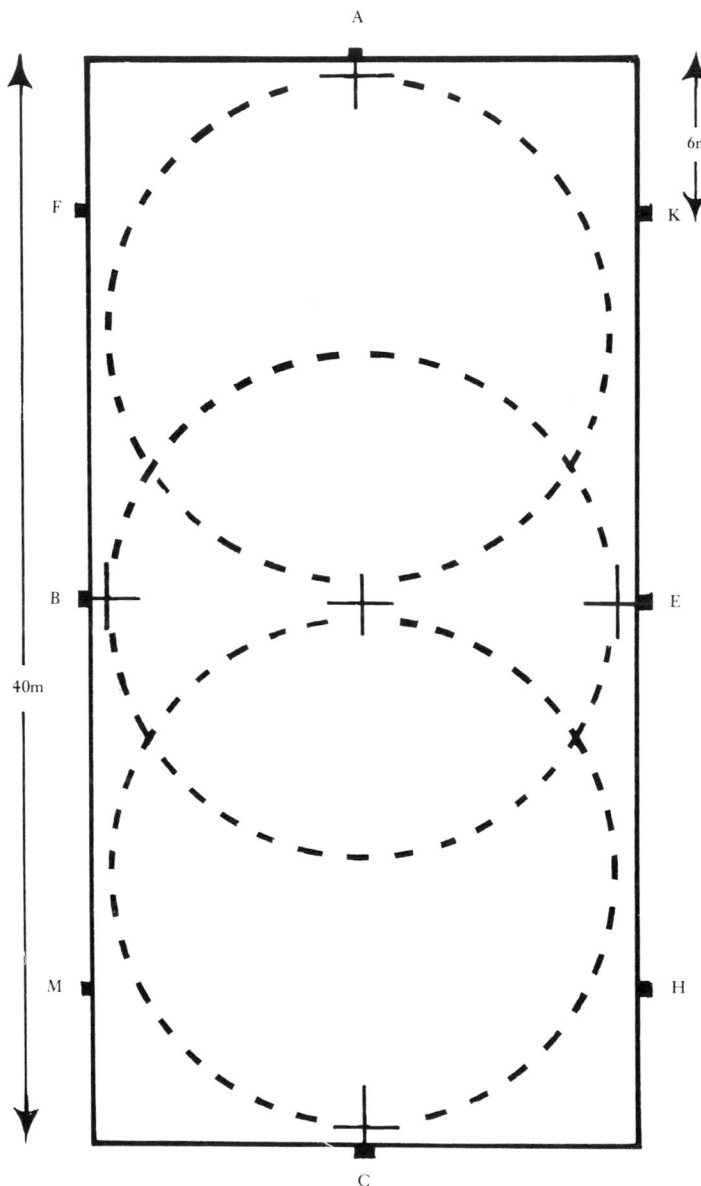

Fig 51   The circles.

but it is only touched for one stride, if it is a circle. When turning off the centre line be careful not to swing off it – this problem is usually caused by the rider swinging one way before the horse turns the other. It is important when doing circles that the outside leg should be drawn back on the open part of the circle, to stop the horse from swinging his quarters out. The horse's hind legs should track in the prints of the front feet and for this to happen the horse must be ridden with both legs into both reins in the rider's hands. Turning down the centre line employs the same basic technique and, as with any movement, it is important to prepare early so that the turn is in the right place and on the centre line, without the quarters swinging.

When changing rein you need to use a straight diagonal and must ensure that this movement is not too close to the corner when arriving at the quarter marker – in this way, the corner itself can be used correctly.

In the dressage test the poorest movement of many horses is the long rein walk which all too often lacks any real stretch and purpose. When the horse really stretches down in this movement it is a clear indication that he is being ridden correctly. It means that he is moving forward to the hands when the reins are given. If the horse keeps his head up and does not lower and stretch, this will demonstrate that he has been kept in position by the hand. The walk should be worked on in the training as the first basic movement. It is an important platform for schooling the horse as, if there is clearly a real stretch in the walk and canter, it shows that the horse is using his back muscles correctly.

The Serpentine

The serpentine is a good movement to work on, as it entails making three even loops, with a change of bend each time; where the rider changes the diagonal each time if in rising trot, the direction is changed. It is necessary to carry this movement out in trot and canter to test the horse's suppleness and his ability to make flowing and continual changes of direction in a balanced manner at pace. With the serpentine it is important to prepare for each change of direction, otherwise these can interfere with the horse's rhythm and balance, stopping his natural movement. It is advisable to start with small loops off the track, ensuring that the bend of the horse stays correct throughout the movement. Gradually these loops can be increased in size. To begin with, start this exercise in trot and only introduce canter after a time. Counter canter is attempted in this way by making small loops off the track of 3–5m, and when the horse is in canter, the centre loop becomes counter canter.

The Basic Paces

Walk

When learning to ride a horse it is important to understand all about the basic paces and their variants. The ordinary walk is at a marching pace and is in four beats which can be counted as the horse is ridden round the arena: near hind, near fore, off hind, off fore. There are five different walks and the same pace should be maintained throughout. The *working walk* is the horse's natural pace. The *free walk* is where the horse walks on a long rein and lengthens and stretches down, displaying complete relaxation. The hands should move forward lightly with the movement of the walk. They must be straight and should only be lowered briefly if the horse starts to lose concentration. The free walk on the loose rein means simply that there is no direct contact between the rider's hands and the horse's mouth, other than through the weight of the reins.

The *medium walk* is the pace between collected and extended walk. The *collected walk* is slower than the medium, with shorter and higher steps. The head approaches the vertical position and therefore the head and neck are raised, while the hind feet do not over-track the prints left by the forefeet. The rhythm

and tempo are maintained by the sensitive influence of the rider's legs and hands. This is a difficult movement and fairly advanced, as is the *extended walk*, where the horse takes longer steps, covering as much ground as possible with each stride, and where the hind feet over-track the print left by the forefeet on the same side. The outline of the horse should appear to lengthen, with the head and neck stretching forward, and there should be definite forward impulsion; the horse must, however, remain on the bit.

Trot

In the *trot* the pace is two beats to a stride, familiarly known as 'two-time'. The horse springs from one diagonal pair

(a)

(b)

Fig 52   Good outlines for a working walk.

of legs to the other with a moment of suspension between each step. The sequence is: near hind and off fore together, then off hind and near fore. A good trot is where the movement is free and active and care must be taken to keep the steps regular and even. Common faults are when the tempo is too fast and the horse runs, or when it is too slow and the trot is not properly established. As with the walk there are different speeds of trot: *collected*, *working*, *medium* and *extended*.

At *working trot* the pace is between medium and collected and is the basic movement and most natural pace for the horse. The *collected trot* is where the steps are shorter and higher, the *medium* is slightly stronger with larger steps, as the horse lengthens its stride and covers more of the ground. The *extended trot* is where the stride pattern is lengthened and can only be executed if the horse is well balanced, with the hind quarters carrying the weight and the hind legs engaged, under the horse's body. The lengthened strides at Novice level for a young horse should be few and give the impression of a difference.

Canter

The *canter* is a pace of three-time, with a silent beat when all feet are off the ground in suspension. The sequence for a horse leading with the off leg should be: near hind, off hind and near fore together, near

Fig 53 *An incorrect position in walk, with the horse very much above the bit.*

Fig 54 *Collected walk, with the horse too short in the neck.*

Fig 55 *Restricted walk with incorrect outline, short in the neck and with the poll high.*

Fig 56 *A good outline and seat for a sitting trot.*

Fig 57   A rising trot with a good outline and good steps.

Fig 58   Trotting – the rider is not taking quite enough contact.

Fig 59   Lengthened stride in trot with good outline for a Novice horse.

Fig 60   Give and retake of the rein in trot.

fore. The more complicated variation of this movement is the counter canter where the horse canters off the wrong leg, so that if he is on the right rein he will lead with the near fore or outside leg. The horse's head should be slightly inclined over the leading leg. A common mistake in the canter movement is where the outside hind leg is dragging behind making the pace four-time.

To get the horse to strike off correctly in canter make a half halt, achieve the correct bend, make sure the rider's weight is slightly on the inside seatbone and then apply the inside leg on the girth and the outside leg behind the girth. Use a little leg pressure with the inside hand very slightly raised. To begin with, it is advisable to execute this movement from the trot in the circle. The canter must be executed properly and consistently on one rein before teaching it on the other. It is important that the canter should be energetic and rhythmic with considerable movement of the horse's head and neck, otherwise the horse will break out of this pace and go back to trot. As with the trot there are different speeds of canter, the basic form being the *working canter*. Again, there are also the *collected*, *medium* and *extended* forms.

The Gallop

The ultimate pace, in tempo terms, is the *gallop*. This is four-time, having four beats to the stride, and asks the horse for greater impulsion and speed than the canter. The outline of the horse lengthens, as does the stride, so that the horse is covering the maximum amount of ground. With the right leg leading the sequence is: near hind, off hind, near fore, off fore. Event horses will use the gallop more as a fitness exercise in preparation for steeplechase and cross country, rather than as a discipline. The rider should work hard at his own technique, and learn to ride with shortened stirrups so that there is good contact with the hand and leg, and the body goes with the horse and not against his natural movement.

Variations

Once the basic groundwork has been done in the different paces, you can experiment with the more complicated movements and transitions. In some tests there will be a simple *change of leg at canter*. This is where the horse is brought back from canter to walk for two or three strides and then restarted into canter with the other leg. Another movement that is often called upon is the *rein back*, which should be an equilateral backward movement where the feet are raised and set down, almost simultaneously, by diagonal pairs. It should be done in four separate beats and the feet should be well raised with the hind feet remaining on the previous line. At the Intermediate level you will encounter *shoulder in*. Here the horse is bent around the inside leg of the rider with the horse's inside fore leg passing and crossing in front of the outside leg. The inside hind leg is placed in front of the outside leg. The shoulder-in should be prepared at an angle of around 30° to the direction in which the horse is moving and is on three tracks.

Dressage and good flat work are the basis upon which any riding should be dependent – through this, the real control, enjoyment and understanding of the horse will be achieved. If the ground-

Fig 61   An introduction to shoulder in – this is not quite sufficient for a test.

work is there then, whether you are hunting, at hunter trials, riding out or participating in eventing, the experience will be enhanced and there will be greater sympathy between you and your horse. Perhaps even more relevant is the fact that by riding properly and with knowledge there is less chance of injury to either horse or rider, as the partnership will be established, the aids will be there and the guidance and instructions will be clear. Proper training will also mean that the horse will be ridden with understanding and consideration. Many hunters and racehorses have lost all sensitivity

in their mouth because they have been pulled in by unsympathetic jockeys who see them merely as speed machines for galloping.

In eventing, especially at the Novice level, many competitions can be won through a good dressage score. Certainly, I have never ridden any of my horses at an event before I felt that the flat work experience was really there. In some cases this has meant holding back a promising youngster, but it has also meant that the dressage score I eventually achieve has often provided me with a cushion – even if I lower one show jump, all is not lost and, more often than not, a good score has given me time in hand for the cross country. With a young or inexperienced horse you often need those few extra seconds to give the horse in the final phase. This can make for a pleasurable rather than rushed experience over unfamiliar obstacles. It is for this reason that I find it helpful to know the leading dressage scores in the class, as well as my own, before setting out cross country, as there may have been valuable seconds gained. Make dressage and precise flat work the basis of your riding because both you and your horse will benefit from this discipline.

It was my continual dedication to the quality of my horses' flat work that meant that in 1986 I could take a formerly good Novice eventer and compete effectively with him at dressage. In less than two months, from the end of July 1986 to mid-September 1986, this horse had qualified for three levels at the National Dressage Championships at Goodwood (at Novice, Elementary and Medium). A year later the same horse was doing Advanced Medium tests and being placed – at this level half-passes,

Fig 62　An introduction to the traverse – there should be more angle in the movement for a test.

Fig 63　The traverse and shoulder in are, in turn, introductions to the half-pass. This is a half-pass to the left, showing the bend and the horse crossing over in front.

Fig 64   Half-pass to the left, showing the bend and the horse crossing over behind.

flying changes and pirouettes are called for. Without the basic groundwork over a number of years it would have been impossible to develop this new aspect of my career. It is the time and attention given to the flat work that has enhanced my enjoyment of riding and enabled me to learn even more about dressage skills and techniques.

7 Show Jumping

Show jumping is the phase of eventing that most riders ignore and usually this is to their cost. Certainly, the British mentality seems to be such that many riders just want to race across the countryside jumping obstacles at speed, an attitude that emanates from a history and tradition in hunting. Many riders have appreciated that when the ground is good and weather conditions favourable, events can often be decided on the dressage phase. This has at least led to a far higher standard of riding in the flat work. Show jumping, however, is still often neglected and yet so many events have been won or lost in this phase. When Virginia Leng won her first Badminton in 1985 on Priceless, it was the fact that she had a clear round, while the American Torrance Fleishman Watkins on Finvarra had two fences down and the New Zealander Mark Todd on Charisma one down, that really counted and moved her from third place to first. So often in one day events, too, when the weather is bad or the ground has become either boggy or slippery, the show jumping can alter the whole picture. When each fence down represents 5 penalty points, a stop or a refusal 10, and falling off 20, in a close competition this can mean the difference between winning and being unplaced.

Over the years I have felt very strongly that it is the work my horses have put in at show jumping competitions, and also the time that they have spent with a show jumping trainer, that makes them better and more careful jumpers, even when it comes to cross country. Two immediate benefits seem to accrue from this training work and experience. Firstly, the horses do not rush because they are used to jumping in a controlled manner, and secondly, they will have better technique.

When training a young horse the introduction of the coloured poles should be taken gradually at first, and they should be jumped at a very low height with the guidance of ground lines and trotting poles. As the horse progresses and becomes more accomplished at jumping the poles and accepting them with confidence, the rider can set about ensuring that the horse jumps in the right way with many gymnastic exercises. As in dressage, the key is the relationship between the horse and the rider, and the building up of trust between the pair.

Early Experience

Shows

It is a good idea to take young horses to small indoor shows and let them have the experience of jumping in the clear round first. However, before jumping for the first time in competitions away from home, take the back rails off the practice fence so that the horse learns not to get frightened by making a mistake. Certainly the in-fills (water, flowers, trees) can be quite strange to a young horse and can upset him. It is important that each outing should be an enjoyable exper-

Fig 65 Jumping a wall – the horse is using his head and neck and is good in front.

ience, as this will gradually help to build up the necessary confidence and trust.

In the early stages, never force a young horse or ask him to go over big obstacles too early but take the advancement slowly and surely instead. All too often I have seen a young horse's confidence broken by being frightened. Be careful not to punish for fences down with a whip. Usually this leads to the horse racing into the obstacles at breakneck often open-mouthed and carrying his head high in the air. The top show jumpers can see a stride so clearly, gauging the take-off point to perfection, that they are able to cope with a horse in this state, but it is neither attractive nor is it likely to be conducive to good dressage or an enjoyable cross country ride. What one should aim for is encouraging the horse to think about looking after both himself and the rider, especially when it comes to cross country. This means instilling confidence and trust in the horse.

Naturally, no one horse is the same as the next and, to get the best out of the horse, the rider must understand each horse he or she rides, and learn how to deal with his character. A cocky, arrogant horse is a very different proposition from a horse that 'spooks' at everything and shies away from obstacles. With young horses there will always be ups and downs – one week you think he is the best young horse you have ever had and the next it seems that he can't jump at all, and you are left wondering what he is doing in the yard. The key is to accept this, and stay with the young horse until he has had time to prove his athletic ability. At this stage you can assess whether you have a star or not.

After jumping an inexperienced horse over a clear round course, only progress slowly. This will build confidence in the horse. Obviously some horses will need more of a challenge more quickly than others; holding such a horse back is not a good idea, since it can lead to laziness, where the horse will tend not to pick up and will jump flat. In this instance the horse can quickly move on to the New-comers or the Badminton class. Again, it is the experience and not winning that is important and even if you feel the horse has jumped well (as opposed to jumping a little too big and extravagantly), leave it and don't jump off that day. It is always better to finish on a high note – too many riders, impetuous and impatient for suc-cess, push on until something goes wrong, which will inevitably happen.

At Home

When schooling at home to begin with, the horse should be allowed to trot into little fences with the help of poles placed 2.30m (about 2½ yds) in front of the obstacles to be jumped. This should change gradually so that the horse learns to canter over the ground in the last few strides, and the length should be extended to 2.75m (about 3 yds). Even in the horse's first competitions you should not be worried about letting the horse trot round the corners to allow his balance

and rhythm to be re-established – this will ensure that he is leading with the right leg and is not on his forehand. In this way, the canter steps necessary for the impulsion at take-off will only be present for the last few strides.

Much of the early work is done in the trot which is good discipline and exercise for the horse. When doing show jumping training never try to catch a horse out but always ensure that the distances between fences are correct and not odd. For the young horse doing trotting exercises the distances should be even and easy. In addition to the take-off pole being 2.30m (2½yds) away from the fence, there should be 5.50–5.95m (6–6½ yds) between the first two fences. Over time the horse will have to learn all about varied distances, but in the early stages he should not be encouraged to have too big a stride but rather to be gymnastic. Once the horse starts to canter then you need to think about the length of his stride. Usually, if he is cantering only over the last few strides, 6.40m (about 7yds) between small fences would be enough. Once the fences get bigger then the normal distance between a double should be 7.30m (8yds) in canter. Again, a useful aid for the horse is to lay canter poles 2.75m (3yds) in front of the fence, which will put him in the right place for the take-off. If the stride is wrong, the pole will help to make the horse adjust and find the correct stride to jump from.

It is useful, even in these early days, to do some cross country schooling and hunting or cubbing as this helps the horse to learn to cope with fences that are solid, as well as to accept different terrains and ground conditions. Hunting can be invaluable as a good horse will think about where to place his feet and how to

Fig 66   Using a pole placed before cross pole – the horse is showing a good approach.

cope with all types of going, while the rider can teach him to go forward with the right impulsion.

Once the horse gains in confidence and has started to participate in a few small competitions, time and attention should be given to building off this platform, making the horse do more gymnastic work and further improving the way he is jumping. If a horse is slightly headstrong and always onward-bound, then it is important to shorten his stride and slow down his pace approaching the obstacle. Conversely, if the horse is too careful and spends too long in the air then you will need to jump smaller fences, with an increased distance between each, in order to try to open the horse out. Having

someone knowledgeable on the ground can help considerably in working out the best remedial treatment for each horse. Even the most experienced horses can fall into bad habits and the gymnastic exercises will help sort out these problems or lapses. Basic trotting and cantering schooling into fences will make the horse think again and perhaps be more careful in his jumping. You should aim to have the horse jumping with a round back, using the head and neck and bringing the legs up in the correct manner. With many young horses the front legs will dangle. This can be overcome by shortening the doubles and the distances between jumps, and doing plenty of pole work to make the horse more athletic. Trotting through cavalletti poles on the lunge and then

Fig 67   Jumping crossed poles – the rider is giving too much rein.

Fig 68   Taking better contact – the horse is using his hocks more, to his advantage.

Fig 69   Good position and contact, showing the benefit of more pronounced steps using shoulders and hocks.

riding the horse over poles and small bounce fences helps sharpen his action in front. For the horse that is lazy behind and not neat, the use of wider parallels in a line of fences can help.

Tack

The rider will need to decide what bit the horse goes best in. The plain snaffle used for dressage may not be enough to control the horse if he is strong and rushing into the fences, and there is always the likelihood of having a fence down if the horse is out of control. A stronger bit will help the horse and enable the rider to present the horse as balanced and in control. In show jumping at shows the horse can be ridden in a standing Martingale, but only a running Martingale is allowed in eventing. Neither blinkers nor draw reins are permissible in any form of jumping. The form of the bit and bridle is up to the individual rider, who must determine what is best for his particular horse. Using the shows for trying different tack on the horse is constructive learning for the eventing season ahead.

Most riders will carry a whip in show jumping, although it should only ever be used as a reminder to a horse who shies away from a jump, to ask him to concentrate on the job in hand. While a whip should be used in instances of disobedience, it must never be used to vent fury – this is a cruel, unnecessary and unpleasant sight and any culprit should be reported by the Steward. Furthermore, a whip should never be used near the horse's head or eyes as there is always the potential danger of inflicting an eye injury.

Tips and Advice

There is little doubt that being assisted in preparation by a top show jumper makes eminent sense. In my case, I have been fortunate enough to have regular lessons for both my students and myself from one of Britain's top International show jumpers, and the real benefit has been in the supervision of the exercise and gymnastic work which aids both horse and rider. Additionally, this tutelage has helped my pupils and myself improve our eye for a stride (learning to see the line of take-off coming into a fence). The top show jumpers have marvellous eyes and hardly ever make the mistake of putting their horse wrongly into a fence. This comes from practice and with the experience of jumping a large number of fences and, undoubtedly, the more show jumping you do the easier it is to see a stride.

Another tip that a knowledgeable show jumper can teach even an experienced event rider is how to walk a course correctly. The purpose of walking a course is to look at the line of fences and the distances between them. In the doubles and combinations it is crucial to establish whether the course builder has been clever and made the distances slightly shorter or longer between the fences. Walking the course with an experienced show jumper can provide the right advice and riding instructions. Certainly you need to make sure that the distances between fences are walked and measured. As a guide, even strides will go on four yards, doubles and combinations will be on eight yards, with twelve yards for a two stride double, sixteen yards would be three strides and twenty yards would be four strides. If, however, the distances are slightly longer (perhaps more than

Fig 70 Collecting the horse in preparation for the next fence – looking for a stride.

twenty yards), then you must decide whether to move on quickly from the last fence, in order to find a nice even stride, or to wait for another stride on what is a long four. Where the whole course is built on catch distances then the rider will have to come back after a fence, re-balance, and re-establish the approach for the next fence. Without measuring out the distances you would keep coming and meeting the fence wrongly. There is another way to solve distance problems and that is by using the ring fully, so that the horse is given plenty of time to see the obstacle.

The governing body's rules book will provide the essential dos and don'ts, but there are some very common problems that can be encountered through sheer nervousness. Starting before the bell or whistle has gone leads to instant elimination, as does dismounting before leaving the arena, irrespective of whether this is done to pick up a glove, whip or hat. Riders riding round the course, checking the order of the fences, may forget they have only a minute from the time the bell is sounded before they must start to jump. Another common error seen is a rider failing to go through the finish.

In simple terms you should know the rules and have walked the course at least once, if not twice; you should have run through the order of the course in your mind at least twice, and, ideally, watched two or more riders complete the course (assuming you are not one of the first to go in the class). This is all good preparation and will help you to assess whether your view of the distances is right, and how the course is riding. When going in, you should also check that all poles and planks are solidly in their cups and have

Fig 71   Walking the distance between fences.

not been dislodged by an earlier rider.

Watching other people ahead of you is sensible as it reveals a great deal about the distances, the problems you might encounter, the ground conditions (whether it is holding or testing), as well as the sturdiness of the obstacles themselves. Furthermore, by watching others, you can gauge the speed necessary to get around in the time allowed. If the timing is tight then you can work out where to accelerate and where to cut corners – incurring time faults in show jumping is inexcusable and will prevent participation in a jump off at a show. Every rider makes an avoidable error once, and when it happens it is bitterly disappointing for everyone concerned. Seldom does one ever make the mistake again. One of the saddest moments I can remember was when one of Britain's top riders was in a clear lead at Bramham Three Day Event coming into the final show jumping phase, but then missed a jump and was subsequently disqualified. There is rarely a second chance.

Competition

Warm-up

When a horse is transported to a competition, never take him out of the box and expect him to jump straight away. Whether the horse has already had some work in preparation for the dressage, which comes first in a one day event, or is being presented just for show jumping, will determine just how much of a warm-up will be necessary. At an event only the tack and saddle will need to be changed between dressage and show jumping, and then the horse will be ready to be taken down to the jumping practice area. At a show the horse will need some flat work to loosen him up before jumping and once he is loosened up you should use the practice fence. An important aid for a rider is to have a helper standing by who can control the height of the practice fence. Ideally, start with a cross pole, move on to a small fence to give the horse confidence, and then build up to a straight upright before having a parallel erected. If the practice fences have flags on them, ensure that the jump is taken with the red flag on the right and the white on the left. It is just possible that a strict Steward could eliminate a rider for not complying with this rule.

If the practice fence has been put up for someone else and is too big or too high, resist the temptation to jump it. If something goes wrong and the horse has to be corrected with the use of the whip, this could unsettle his mind, make him nervous and uptight, and lead to an indifferent round. Worse still can happen where a rider is foolish enough to attempt a jump that is considerably higher than any that will be encountered in the ring; the horse may get a fright, slip into it and his legs could become caught up between the poles. When the horse goes into the ring after this, a stop will often follow. Fortunately, in eventing this does not happen, as the height of the practice fence is not allowed to be any higher than the allotted height maximum for the level of event in which the horse is competing.

How many practice jumps you should do and how high the fence should be depends largely on the nature and temperament of the horse. A slightly careless horse may need a bigger fence as a reminder to be careful, and this type of horse should be allowed to knock the

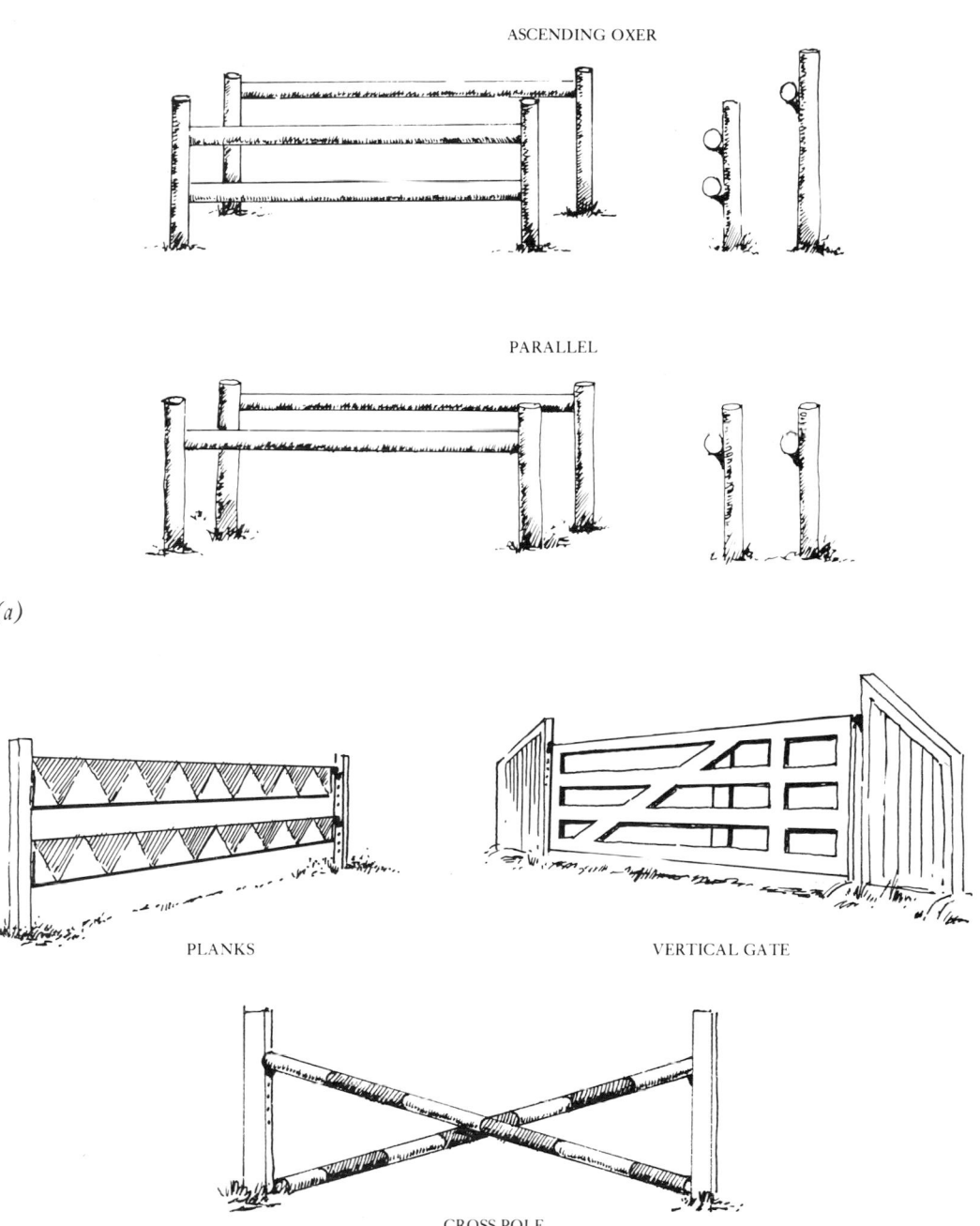

ASCENDING OXER

PARALLEL

(a)

PLANKS

VERTICAL GATE

CROSS POLE

(b)

Fig 72   Examples of show jumps.

fence and even have a pole down. A horse that is slightly stiff may need to jump a few fences to loosen up, while another horse could easily get wound up and over-excited if he is asked to do too much jumping in the collecting ring.

The Jump Off

At a show when jumping, assuming that horse and rider are clear and within the time, they will have qualified for the jump off (or the clear round class). Sometimes there will be justification in going for the jump off as this could sharpen up a horse's basic action and his ability to jump at speed. However, it is not worth cutting corners, going at breakneck speed and upsetting the horse, since this merely undoes the work that has gone into developing his show jumping technique. There is no real reason for an eventer to do this, as in eventing the time is reasonably generous and the objective is simply to get around clear. With an older, more experienced horse with show jumping skill, providing it is undertaken sensibly, there is merit in learning how to turn quickly, and in having an eye on how to jump fences quickly in order to save time, as this can prove to be relevant training for cross country. Nevertheless few of the top show jumpers really gallop at the jumps – they save the time between the fences by turning very quickly and coming inside fences, thus shortening the line to the obstacle.

Jumping at Shows and at Events

There are minor differences between show jumping at shows and this particular phase in eventing:

1. The technique required for show jumping is a combination of agility and speed; in eventing it is basically agility, although timing is a consideration.
2. Ultimately, a show jumper is aiming for a place in a jump off, either against the clock or with higher obstacles; in eventing the goal is just a clear round, but within the time allotted.
3. At a show a fence down is four faults, the first stop three faults, the second six faults and the third elimination; in eventing it is five faults for every fence down, ten faults for the first refusal, twenty for the second and then elimination for the third. Both have time fault penalties.
4. While at shows a standing martingale is allowed; this is not permissible equipment for eventing, although a running martingale may be used.

Practice

Do not be deterred by the fact that some horses go better outdoors rather than indoors – it is still good practice teaching a big horse to negotiate the tight turns and corners of an indoor arena. Naturally, some horses will favour the ground in an indoor arena, but it is important that horses learn to jump both indoors and outdoors.

While learning show jumping technique and practising at shows it is useful to have someone tape the action on video. This will help you to check what is right and wrong about the horse and rider: the seat, the way the horse is being ridden, seeing the right stride, the take-off, the horse's agility and position of legs, and the pace. Analyse the tape carefully, and don't be too quick to blame the horse. It is often the case that if the horse had been ridden better to a fence, the obstacle

Fig 73   Jumping a small upright with the reins a little too long.

Fig 74   Jumping planks – the reins are a little long.

Fig 75   Jumping planks – the horse could use himself more and be better in front.

would have been cleared. While the horse will often get the rider out of trouble he can only really go as well as the way the person rides. With show jumping the key is practice, as an eye for a stride is only developed from jumping many fences. Having the desire and commitment to improve, taking lessons, and watching the experts and trying to learn from them, will all help to make the rider better in this phase. Use the close season and early part of the year to work on show jumping and if things are going badly in this phase during the season, take time out to identify and correct the problems. Sometimes the fault is with the rider, sometimes with the horse, and occasionally with the equipment being used. If the horse is suddenly flat over the obstacles, check

firstly that he is right in his back or that he has not pulled a muscle in his hind quarters, and secondly ensure that he is not 'over the top' and needing a rest.

Where to Compete

Do not just rely on local unaffiliated shows, as the fences at these venues can often be flimsy and insubstantial. Despite the expense, it is well worthwhile registering the horse so that he will be able to compete at recognised and affiliated show jumping competitions. The courses built under rules tend to be more solid while the competition is usually stronger. To begin with there is the Badminton class, an excellent introduction for the young horse, where the fences are only 1m

Jumping a double

Fig 76   Approach.

Fig 77   Still approach.

Fig 78 Jumping the first part.

Fig 79 Jumping the second part.

(3ft 3in) high. The horse will advance from this to the Newcomers class. Once he is jumping really well and is being aimed at Intermediate or Advanced levels in eventing we can progress to Foxhunters. The fence height and type of course at Foxhunters level are fairly similar to those encountered in the higher echelons of eventing. This top level practice means that there will be no unpleasant surprises when the horse, or indeed the rider, comes to doing his first Intermediate event. Horses may only compete in some classes until they have won a certain amount of prize money, otherwise they must partake as *Hors Concours* competitors. For would-be event horses, and by way of a change, there is a very useful competition in Britain, sponsored by Spillers Horsefeed. This incorporates the combined training of dressage and show jumping (with both a Novice and Open category), and the final takes place at The Horse of the Year Show at Wembley, in October. The Novice class is equivalent to a Novice level of dressage and a difficult level of show jumping in a Novice event, while the Open class represents the equivalent of Elementary level for dressage and Intermediate height for show jumping (at a registered Horse Trial).

Despite the reputation that show jumpers have had in the past for not paying sufficient attention to getting their horses' basic paces right, nor doing enough flat work, and even in some cases employing fairly crude methods in order to make their horses jump higher and cleaner, many good event horses have emerged from show jumping backgrounds. Certainly, there is much encouragement to be gained from riding a horse that has been a good and natural show jumper, as they are often clever enough to get a rider out of trouble when meeting a fence wrongly.

It is not simply due to a lack of events that the most successful event riders are seen winning Novice, Foxhunter and Newcomer classes at show jumping events indoors and outdoors in the off season. The horses themselves greatly benefit from travelling to shows, getting on and off the horse-box, learning to settle and, when sufficiently experienced, taking part in jump offs. This practice is invaluable and it is important preparatory work for the events to come, as the horse is schooled and can establish the right way of jumping before being expected to take on cross country fences at pace. The top riders do not make the mistake of going cross country before getting the rudiments of show jumping into their horse's mind and action. Many event horses lose their jump because poor riders ask them to jump fences quickly across country before they have the jumping technique correct. The result of making this mistake is that the horse will tend to rap the fences, while in the show jumping he will be flat, taking poles and planks with him. In a Novice event where there is often a span of only five or six marks between the first six horses, one fence down in the show jumping phase, and the resultant five penalty points, could prove to be the difference between winning and losing.

8 Cross Country

Schooling

For any would-be event horse or rider the cross country schooling is something that has to be taken very seriously, and should be treated neither recklessly or lightheartedly. There are many young riders who go to their first event without having done any cross country schooling and are then surprised when they get into trouble at obstacles different from anything they have faced before. Another mistake often made by the over-exuberant rider is treating schooling as though it is the main event, and galloping needlessly over obstacles, often unsupervised, at breakneck speed and with no care for his own safety or for that of the horse. Seldom will this kind of performance lead to a happy and confident horse who is sound throughout the season.

It is absolutely essential for the horse to have sufficient cross country schooling, and to learn to jump naturally over every type of fence that he will be expected to negotiate in competition. It is important, too, for the horse and rider to go to different venues to get experience of different combinations, terrains and fence structures. Hunting and hunter trials will also aid the preparation and provide invaluable experience for a potential event horse. Hunting is a great advantage in that it teaches the horse to find his feet in all kinds of weather and ground conditions, plus it gives him the experience over natural obstacles. However, there is no substitute for training over the man-made fences encountered on the cross country course. The horse must learn how to jump into water, over water, ditches, walls, gates, downhill fences, uphill fences, through a coffin, a bounce and combinations, as well as into a darkened area (such as over a fence going into a wood). It is also important to school the horse over such obstacles as angled fences and corners. The only way to know the horse's strengths and weaknesses is by experimentation.

However, none of this should be considered or undertaken until the basic fitness work has been done and this means that the vital canter work and galloping will have been under way for at least four weeks prior to the first event. When going cross country schooling, always loosen or warm the horse up, and give horse and rider a feel of the ground conditions, and a couple of preparatory jumps over small fences, before tackling bigger obstacles or water jumps.

Different Cross Country Fences

Again, if you have done your homework through the winter and the horse has learnt how to show jump properly, and completed his gymnastic and exercise work suggested by the show jumping fraternity, he should be ready to be schooled over solid obstacles. On a cross country schooling there should be a range of fences that will test the horse's

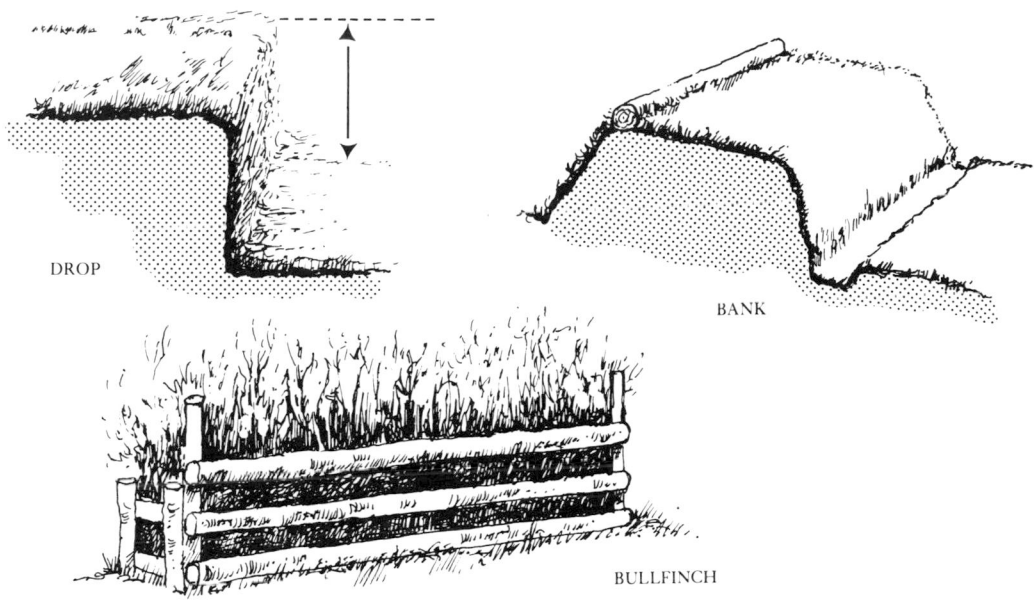

DROP

BANK

BULLFINCH

(a)

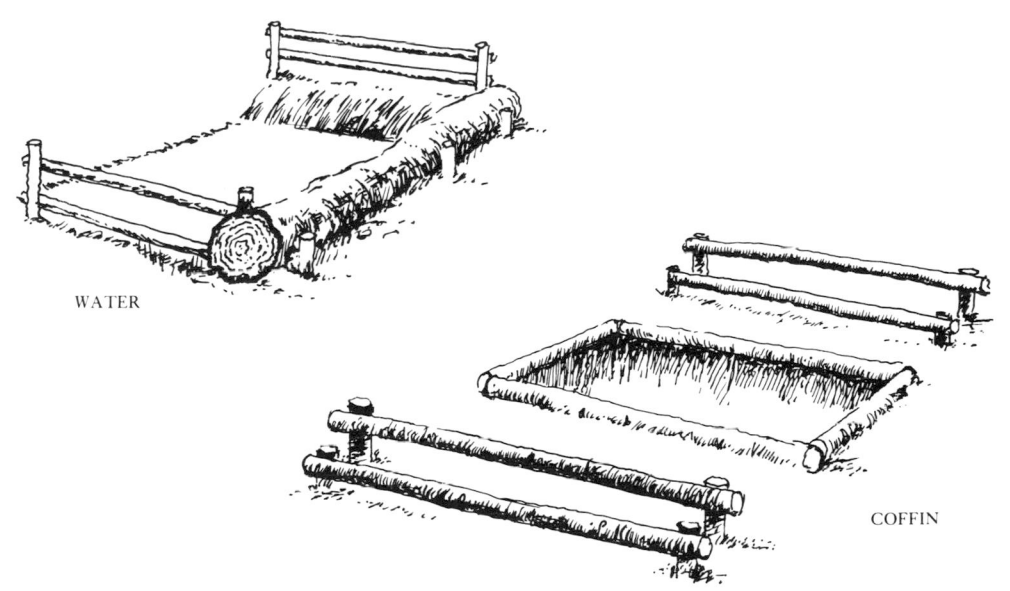

WATER

COFFIN

(b)

UPRIGHT

TRIPLE BAR

TIGER TRAP/TRAKHENER (WITH DITCH UNDERNEATH)

(c)

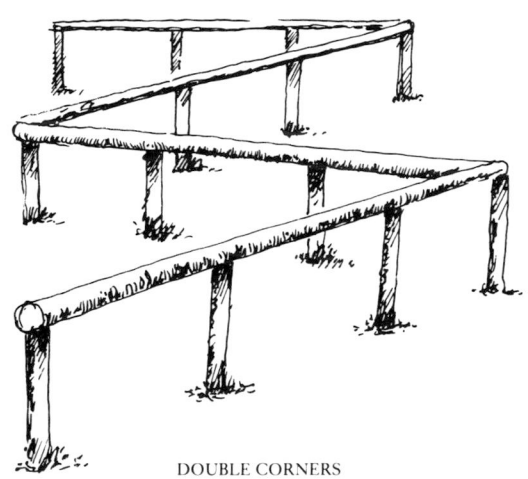

DOUBLE CORNERS

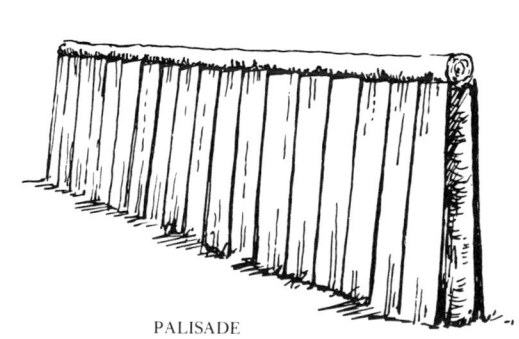

PALISADE

(d)

HANGING LOG

(e)

Fig 80 Examples of cross country fences.

ability to stand off, or, alternatively, to get in close. For example, a fence with an open ditch in front will require the horse to come into it at a fairly strong gallop, standing off the fence in order to clear both ditch and rail. On the other hand, when jumping into water the horse does not want to come in too fast – if he stands off and makes a big leap, the chances are that he may lose his balance. As a novice rider, learn to jump conservatively into water, rather than to launch yourself in.

It is not by chance that the 'Lake' at Badminton and the 'Trout Hatchery' at Burghley so often cause most of the problems on the course, while attracting the biggest crowds. The difficulty is that, at International level, there is usually an obstacle before that has to be negotiated, making the entry into the water doubly difficult. The impulsion needed to get over the obstacle may force the rider to jump too big, and as a result the horse sees the drop into water too late and, in his shock, finds himself unable to get the 'landing gear' down in time. If you go a fraction too slowly into the obstacle, the horse may not be able to jump the fence cleanly, and this can result in the rider being tipped out of the saddle as the horse

struggles to find his legs. The water complexes at Lexington and Gawler World Championships caused untold problems, and there were some particularly nasty falls at the bounce in the water at Gawler.

When you come to open water which has to be cleared (as opposed to jumping in) your approach should be at a strong gallop, encouraging the horse to lengthen his stride and jump out, as opposed to jumping in when the pace has to be much more controlled. Schooling in and over water is essential, since this is a hazard encountered in many events. The horse must learn to accept water and getting wet, and must be taught not to fear it because the bottom surface cannot be seen. This involves trust and practice as much as anything else for both the horse and the rider.

Upright fences such as gates require careful riding because galloping into them and missing a stride can suddenly result in horse and rider being turned over. The horse needs to be balanced and it is as well to think of an upright as one would a show jump.

A common problem encountered at an event is where the horse has to jump from

Jumping a bank with a ditch in front followed by rails, involving a bounce stride

Fig 81   Approach to bank.

Fig 82   Take-off, showing strain put on hocks during cross country jumping – event horses must have good hocks to be able to stand this.

Fig 83   Jumping on to the bank.

Fig 84   Take-off for the rails.

Fig 85   Landing after the rails.

Fig 86   Introducing a young horse to water, letting him follow
the lead of an experienced horse.

Fig 87   Rewarding the horse with a pat after introducing him to water.

Fig 88   First lesson – jumping off one step into water.

Jumping steps into water

Fig 89   The first step.

Fig 90   Approach to the second step, showing good position.

*Fig 91   Over the second step and approaching the water,
showing good contact using legs, hands and seat.*

Fig 92   Entering the water, keeping balanced.

Fig 93   Moving through the water.

Fig 94   Maintaining balance and good contact all the way through.

Jumping through a coffin

Fig 95   Approach.

Fig 96   Jumping log.

Fig 97 Landing after log.

Fig 98 Approach to second part – the ditch.

Fig 99   Jumping the ditch.

Fig 100   Approach to final part – the post and rails.

Fig 101   Jumping rails.

Fig 102   Landing.

light into darkness or where he has to come out of gloom into bright light. In this situation the horse is unable to see clearly where he is going and may put in an abrupt stop. The rider must recognise this and bring the horse back, balance him and make a strong and direct approach, so that he takes confidence from the fact that the rider seems to know where to go.

Most event courses will have a coffin and this can easily frighten a young horse, especially if he jumps too big over the first element and gets too close to the second element. To avoid this, teach the horse over a coffin with a small first element, letting him see where he is going – the rider must be positive in the approach. Even in competition this fence should be respected by the rider and approached at the correct pace.

Combination fences need to be approached at the same angle at which the rider intends to jump them allowing the horse to move easily from the first part to the second part, and then on. When walking the course, evaluate whether the distances in the combination are short or long, and this will determine the speed at which to approach the fence.

With bounce fences (becoming more and more popular, even at the Novice level), you need to come in with enough impulsion and rhythm so that the horse lands over the first part like a spring that is still coiled, and then leaps over the second, rather like the coiled spring releasing itself. To achieve this, the contact with the reins and legs must be strong and secure. At a higher level double bounces will be encountered, and here the

Jumping a bounce fence

Fig 103 Approach.

Fig 104   *Jumping first part.*

Fig 105   *Jumping second part.*

necessary impulsion is even greater. Care must be taken, however, to ensure that the horse does not jump flat and long, otherwise he will go chest first into the second element and not pick up sufficiently to negotiate the fence properly.

Training over uphill and downhill fences is essential as courses are often built on hilly country, especially in Britain. Gawler Park in Australia where the World Championships took place in 1986 was a good example of a long course with a strong incline towards the end; considerable rainfall before the event resulted in very testing ground, which led to a number of horses (even some of the British contingent, with their strong reputation for fitness) finishing very tired. Naturally, few courses in a normal season would be anywhere near as demanding, but uphill and downhill fences will still be

encountered even at a preliminary Novice event. An uphill fence needs approaching with enough impulsion so that the horse can push and take off with the hocks underneath. The downhill fences need to be jumped more slowly so that the horse is balanced and not running on to the forehand. If it is taken slowly the horse has time to balance himself into the jump.

Corner fences and angles must be approached accurately and the rider must have a clear line of direction. It is a good idea when walking the course to find a line or mark on the horizon to aim at when riding a corner or an angle.

Banks that have to be jumped on to and off require sufficient impulsion, but can be jumped at any pace, depending on the height.

Fig 106   Jumping a corner fence.

Fig 107   Jumping up a bank out of water.

Fig 108   Take-off at the second bank.

Riding Technique

Your riding technique across country is very important, in that it is critical to ride in a way that is a help to the horse. When Lester Piggott rode on the flat, it was with his backside high in the air in order to take the weight off the horse's back, and he relied on his poise, balance and skill to steer the horse and to ride so many memorable finishes. Similarly, over the hurdles and even over chase fences, Andy Turnell would ride very short to avoid sitting heavy on the horse's back; this was very effective, although from time to time, if the horse hit the fence hard, he was in danger of being catapulted out of the saddle. Event riders should ride with long stirrups and leathers for dressage, so that the position is right and they are sitting deep into the saddle, with shorter ones for the show jumping, that still enable the horse to have maximum assistance, and as short as is comfortable and balanced for cross country. When the horse is galloping the rider should be out of the saddle and going with him, while taking the weight off his back. With difficult fences, the rider must be athletic and try to stay with the horse's movement.

Fitness

In order to have a good and effective riding technique the rider needs to be just as fit as the horse. A fit rider will always be more alert and able to react quickly. An unfit rider is a hindrance to the horse. Regular exercise such as swimming, walking or jogging can all help to strengthen the muscles and again it is in the close season that this work should be undertaken. Riding daily will help, but

Fig 109 Galloping across country. The rider's weight is out of the saddle and both the horse and rider are well balanced.

does not necessarily strengthen all the muscles. Your position and balance can be improved by working on your shoulders, back and stomach muscles, and swimming regularly can help enormously. Ride from time to time without stirrups, and do exercises as this will help the seat and inside thigh muscles. Anything that will help conserve the horse when going cross country is worthwhile, and improved strength, balance and fitness all enable you to take the weight off the back of the horse more easily.

Rhythm

The correct way to ride a course is to get into a rhythm and to establish the right seat for cross country riding. The pace should be consistent. The inexperienced rider who gallops flat out between fences, and takes a long time slowing down in preparing to meet the fence, will not achieve a fast time. It is the horse who is well trained and schooled, who can decrease or accelerate his pace evenly and without fighting or wasting time, who will have the faster round.

Thinking Ahead

Valuable seconds can be gained by thinking and looking ahead, thereby taking the shortest route to the following fence. Correct balance of both horse and rider on landing over an obstacle will not only save time but also conserve the horse's energy. There are two important considerations that have to be taken into account: firstly, which is the optimum route, and secondly, how the fence is going to jump. The quick route is not always the best or safest. Certainly, where there is an alternative the prudent option may be best, especially for a young horse, even though it may be costly in terms of time. The fences are designed to encourage riders to take the quickest, most direct route, but this route will be more difficult than the alternatives. Walking the course will establish the correct route to take as well as the best way to jump the fence. Often in a big competition the experienced riders will walk the course twice (three or four times in the case of a three day event) in order to establish firmly the way each fence should be jumped, where the approach

should be made, how many strides should be taken and what part of the fence to jump. It is then necessary to consider where the landing will take the horse in terms of the direction of the next fence. Always assess the alternative route you might take, should the horse not be going well on the day or in case the fence is found not to be riding well.

Another important factor to be taken into consideration when walking a course is how it will hold up to weather conditions, especially if the ground is very soft and the rain is still falling. Additionally, not only will different event courses suit some horses better than others, but they will also necessitate different riding tactics. A bold, galloping course encourages good jumping and results in the horse flowing on. A twisty and more difficult course will require more respect and care needs to be taken in the approach to the fences. If the course has become wet and boggy there will be places where the rider must slow down, in order to avoid slipping into a fence or falling by trying to gallop through a bog. Conversely, when the ground is rock hard, at the height of the summer, the rider needs to evaluate whether the ground is flat and safe without ruts, and whether the length of the grass is sufficient to encourage a fast pace. If the ground is uneven and hard, perhaps with little lush grass, it is probably advisable to go at a more sedate pace and save the horse for another day.

If your preparation has been done properly, and every aspect and eventuality has been considered, then the element of risk is less and it becomes a matter of calculated decision rather than a gamble. Experience has taught me that taking

Jumping a fence with a ditch in front

Fig 110   A reasonable approach. The rider's lower leg could be more secure, with the heel down.

Fig 111   Take-off – the rider is in front of the movement with the reins too long.

Fig 112   The rider is still too far forwards and the reins are too long.

Fig 113   The rider's lower leg could be more secure and the heel down.

*Fig 114   Jumping hedge – the horse is in a good position
and the rider is well balanced.*

*Fig 115   Jumping a parallel – the rider's position and
technique are correct.*

chances can come off once but seldom twice, and invariably it is the horse that comes to grief. I have learnt over the years not to be foolish and take risks, but to prepare beforehand, and then ride the course thoughtfully, safely and accurately. It is the approach to the fence that is absolutely vital and this will determine whether the obstacle is negotiated successfully or not. The rider will develop an eye for this over time, and with the benefit of plenty of experience.

Rules

As in every other phase of eventing you must know the rule book. In three day eventing, for example, you will need to know where the penalty zones around a fence begin and end, as there is no penalty if you fall off the horse outside this defined area. Bear in mind that in a one day event there are no penalty zones and therefore if you fall off in front of a fence, or if the horse jumps you off but you hang on for a few strides, the chances are that the jump judge would penalise you 60 points on the grounds that this happened while you were negotiating the fence.

If you are fortunate enough to be leading after the dressage and show jumping at a one day event, you should determine how many seconds you have in hand for the cross country, as this can spare the horse having to gallop needlessly. Every three seconds over the optimum time is a time fault, while every new four-second period is another time fault. This can encourage a rider to take a time-consuming alternative at a difficult obstacle, rather than chancing a fall which is 60 penalty points, or a run out or a refusal (both 20 penalty points). Be careful of over-enthusiastic supporters – while it is permissible for a rider who has fallen to be helped back into the saddle by an outsider, or even to have the horse caught and the tack reassembled and held by a spectator, 'outside assistance' is strictly forbidden. This normally relates to a member of the rider's support team passing information on during their cross country round about times or a particular fence that seems to be catching riders out. If a fence judge or steward believes that outside assistance has been given, the horse and rider will automatically be eliminated. It is up to the rider alone to work out the timings, the best direction and the safest way to take a fence.

Should you suffer the ignominy of a fall, the first thing to do is to check the horse, making sure that he is sound. Start off in trot to make sure the horse is sound. If you are in any doubt and suspect temporary lameness or a trapped nerve, you must retire. When you are eliminated or forced to retire in eventing you are not permitted to jump another fence and the stewards are very strict on this because you are potentially in danger of impeding the next competitor. The following rider has right of way over any competitor ahead who has had a fall, is eliminated or has retired.

On the Day

Before riding cross country make sure there is sufficient time to loosen the horse up by walking, trotting and cantering and possibly even giving him a short gallop. Once all appears well, jump a couple of practice fences (usually available near to the start of the cross country

Fig 116   Jumping a hedge – the horse is jumping flat and is not neat in front.

phase), so that the horse realises what is coming up and can mentally attune.

Ride with purpose and determination to the first fence, and avoid making the mistake that many riders have made over the years, of riding passively to the first fence. The horse will often stop, not realising that this is the cross country phase and not the dressage. If, for one reason or another, there is a hold-up at the start, make sure the horse is kept warm and have a rug available. Do not stand still as the cold will make the horse stiffen up. Similarly, if the Steward stops you on the course, keep the horse moving and register the length of the delay on the stop-watch so that any dispute over time can be argued with supporting evidence.

When riding cross country do not take even the smallest fence for granted as this will invariably be the one to cause you trouble. Treat every fence with respect and count the fences in your mind so that you do not miss any out. I have often walked round with a friend or owner and then tested my memory on the order of the fences. It is extremely disappointing, and needless, to feel you have completed a good round, only to discover a capital 'E' for elimination on the board because you missed out a fence or even an extra loop out in the country. Even now I try to follow the numbers to make sure I am jumping the fences in the correct order.

Keep concentrating right through to the finish and avoid rushing the last fence in the excitement of getting round – treat it with the same respect as any other fence on the course. Remember to go through the finish line and then let the horse slow down gradually, maintaining an even contact on the reins so that there is little danger of the horse being injured by stopping suddenly. Inexperienced riders are so often seen galloping through the finish on a long flapping rein, and it is always a sign of poor riding. When the horse has been pulled up at the end of the course, the rider should get off and walk the horse back to the box.

Once back at the box the horse should be washed down completely, and all the sweat marks removed, and then, if the weather is warm, he can be walked dry. His legs should be bandaged and it is sometimes advisable to use a cooling lotion on the legs. The horse should be kept warm after the event, and on a cold spring or autumn day you must sponge him down quickly, removing the saddle and sweat marks on the neck, and then put a rug on (over the loins in particular) or blankets with a rug on top. The horse can be groomed properly when he is back in the stable.

Depending on how hot the day is the horse should have either a sweat sheet or a thermal rug through which his skin can still breathe; this will enable him to dry out and keep warm at the same time. When he is sufficiently dry the horse should be rugged up so he is warm and comfortable.

Once the competition is over the horse should be given a small drink of water, but this must be carefully controlled and only a few mouthfuls allowed at a time. Too much water on an empty stomach can easily cause colic. After a little water on a perfect summer's day, the horse should be allowed to graze for a short while.

After grazing, or when completely dry (at least one hour after the cross country has finished), the horse should be given more water and then a small feed; this should be of a laxative nature with bran in it so that it is not too hard for him to digest. After this he can have a hay net and water.

While you are grooming the horse after cross country look for any cuts, scrapes or rub marks and deal with these immediately. Pick out the feet, and remove the studs before returning home to avoid the horse doing an injury either to himself or to a travelling companion. If one of the shoes is twisted, remove it, because it is all too easy for a horse to scrape or cut himself with an ill-fitting shoe.

Should there be a deep cut, or if the horse appears to have a chill or colic, call the vet on duty at the event immediately. It is always better to be safe than sorry.

When competing at an event for the first time, remember that you are educating the horse for the future. The speed you choose to go at will depend both on the conditions and on the age, temperament and experience of the horse. Some riders will know whether the horse is ready to go at the desired speed or whether he is unable to do so and jump the fences safely and well. With most horses it will pay to take it more slowly and gain good experience for both of you.

When you have completed the event, irrespective of how you have done you should go and watch the other more experienced competitors to see how they tackle a fence that may have caused you

Fig 117 Jumping a stile – the horse is too low in the shoulder, and is not neat in front.

Fig 118 Jumping a stile – the horse is dangling his legs and therefore is not jumping well.

problems or been difficult to ride. If the course has not ridden well, or if, on reflection, you decide that a number of fences were slightly chancy, and you were lucky to get away with it, go out into the country and watch a top rider tackle the same fence. You never stop learning, and it is good to watch others as it helps you analyse where you went wrong. Even when I have won I have gone out to watch other riders afterwards as I accept that there is always something to glean from observation – perhaps even more so in cross country riding than in any other phase of eventing. Lucinda Green, probably one of the best cross country riders of the modern age, and Virginia Leng, arguably the most complete rider across all phases, are often exemplary in the way they ride a course. It is interesting to note, too, how much credit they give to the horse. Virginia Leng's grey, Murphy Himself (only 8 years old at the time) was given a ride round Burghley in autumn 1986 that was so beautifully judged in pace and accuracy that she was able to achieve an historic fourth successive victory there.

9 The First Event

Before the First Event

General Fitness

Getting the horse fit and ready for competition is really a matter of timing. Some riders prefer not to go for the very early events, which are often affected by adverse conditions, ranging from snow to blustery icy winds, heavy cold rain or sleet. Others, however, have to get their horses ready right at the start of the season, because of the Badminton Horse Trials in early spring. The spring events start officially in mid-March, therefore, if they are to be considered, the horses will need to be back in work immediately after Christmas and should be shod and ready for preparation no later than January 1st. Naturally, if the horse has been hunting he will already have a certain amount of fitness but even so, ten weeks should be allowed to prepare him for the first event of the season.

Always be careful when starting to get a horse fit – if he has been let down and is not in condition he could be carrying excess weight, and any strenuous work too early can lead to both heart and leg strains, causing irreparable damage. Depending on what he has been doing, walking may be the most he should do in the early stages if he is very unfit and overweight. This will start to harden the legs, turn the fat into muscle and bring the horse's condition back. In these instances, only walking is recommended over the first few days, and after ten days, this can be increased to one and a half hours hacking on the roads. After about a fortnight, a short period of schooling can gradually be introduced after the walking, increasing from ten to fifteen minutes up to half an hour. The horse will obviously sweat, but the rider must ensure that he is not being overworked or becoming distressed in these early stages. Personally, I do not like to see horses allowed to grow too fat in their off season – this can put an unnecessary strain on their heart and legs. Larger hunters are especially likely to suffer from being turned out for a long spell in the summer, since with the lush grass they can put on weight very quickly.

When the horse has been back in training for a couple of weeks the hacking work can include some trotting. This should be carried out on the verge so that there is little risk of the horse becoming jarred up by the hard ground – certainly, if the horse has had splints or leg trouble you should not trot on the road itself. If there are places where the horse can trot uphill at this stage of his fitness training, so much the better, as this helps to strengthen his muscles while getting him to use his hocks. Because hill work is more strenuous, a shorter riding time will be necessary than if the terrain around the stables is very flat.

Once the first month is behind you, the horse can start to be schooled for longer, with a little jumping and basic dressage being introduced. At the six week stage this can be further advanced to include some gentle canter work. Initially, this should be for no more than four minutes in a large field or on the gallops, and the rider should shorten the stirrups as though riding across country. The horse's speed should be controlled and he must not be allowed to get uptight or to work too fast in pace. Only with regular cantering should the speed and the duration increase.

To start with, the four-minute canters at a sensible speed should take place every third or fourth day. After a couple of weeks you can move on to two four-minute canters with three minutes of walking between each. This will help the rider to determine the recovery rate and the fitness of the horse. It is advisable to precede the canter with trot work, starting with five minutes and building up to ten minutes. This is good training for the roads and tracks phase that is encountered in all two and three day events. It also helps the horse to settle. Eventually you can build up to one five-minute canter at three-quarter speed and then two five-minute canters – this is the most that a novice horse would ever be expected to do. If the terrain is hilly then one canter uphill for five minutes would probably suffice. More experienced horses will do two five-minute spells and on the final canter prior to an event would go for a short distance at the speed required for the cross country.

Depending on the temperament of the horse, cantering is done either alone or in pairs. An easily excitable horse usually canters on his own, while a lazy horse should be given the lead by a strong canterer to encourage him to work harder. To teach control at the canter it is advisable to start off at a reduced pace, build up speed and then decrease the pace,

so that the changes in pace become smooth and natural, rather than resisted or forced by the rider. This simple exercise should ensure that the horse learns to settle and work in a rhythm, finding galloping effortless. The more time a horse spends fighting with the rider on the cross country course the more stamina he is using, while wasting valuable time. A simple calculation to keep in mind is that for every pull a rider takes a second has been wasted. Arguing about the pace with a horse can, therefore, cost the partnership the event.

It is critical that cantering should only be carried out on good ground. This is not always easy to find in Great Britain, where early in the spring or late in the autumn there is either snow or a frost, and where in the summer the ground can become very hard. Always miss a canter rather than go on unfit ground, as this can either lame the horse, or result in him pulling a tendon or a muscle. Ideally, try to find some all-weather gallops, box the horses up and take them there.

It is essential to remember that with horses speed can kill – never race a horse in training, and if he has had any serious leg trouble you should certainly not work him at too fast a pace. For the same reason you should always give the horse every chance and plenty of time by doing as much slow work as possible in the early training periods. Hills help considerably, not only for fittening work and strengthening the lungs, heart and wind, but also because training on them means that the fast work can be reduced appreciably.

A horse that is advanced can take more work, and indeed may need to be worked twice a day, with an hour in the morning and an hour in the afternoon – this is preferable to doing two hours in one spell. Most horses will work better with two shorter periods rather than one long one and the morning's training could involve a hack while the afternoon could concentrate on dressage schooling.

Variation in the Routine

As the horse progresses towards his first event each day's work should be varied considerably. On some days there should be a canter and on others (usually once a week), a jumping session. A routine that seems to work is as follows: if the horse has been to a show jumping or dressage competition at the weekend, let him have the Monday off; Tuesday could then be slow work and schooling on the flat; on Wednesday there should be more schooling and a little canter work; Thursday will be canter work; Friday, schooling and jumping; Saturday, a canter, and Sunday would take in another small local competition, either for dressage or show jumping.

Jumping Preparation

While it is accepted that too few riders give enough time to their basic flat work, it is also true to say that gaining sufficient show jumping experience in the training is often a problem. Too many event riders believe that hunting and hunter trials are the best and most relevant experience. What they fail to realise is that show jumping practice and experience make up the horse's gymnastic work, and that this will teach a horse to be supple and clever even when it comes to the tricky fences going cross country. It is important when doing show jumping at home to use coloured fences, and to

seek advice from experts who will probably recommend that you ultimately attend some shows. So often in the major competitions we have seen up-and-coming riders fall out of the reckoning because of a weak show jumping phase. In three day events these lapses are often caused by tiredness or stiffness in the horse after a day of gruelling roads and tracks, steeplechase and cross country, but still the show jumps on the third day are there to be negotiated.

A young horse can only benefit from the experience of shows and this should help build reliability in this phase at Novice events. It can be trying and testing to wait at show jumping events, be they Badminton, Newcomers, Foxhunters or Novice classes, often with as many as sixty competitors in each class, but it is important homework that can pay real dividends in a tight competition later in the season. Many of my wins in one day events came from gaining a good dressage score, jumping clear in the show jumping phase when the ground was tacky and holding and the fences flimsy, and then being in the comfortable position of not having to gallop fast round the cross country course in order to secure the win. Most of the top riders have done a fair amount of show jumping in their lives, not only during the winter, but also during periods when they are not eventing, such as in the middle of summer.

It is critically important, however, not to frighten the horse by asking too many questions and jumping too big fences. Try to find a course that is likely to represent the standard of show jumps encountered at a Novice or Intermediate event, so that the horse's attention and concentration will be on his technique and not his height or speed. In the training at home the horse should also be loose jumped over fences as this will start to make him judge his stride and make him more careful. This could prove to be invaluable – the horse will learn how to get himself out of trouble.

This cautionary advice about jumping obstacles sensibly and not trying to be ambitious applies even more closely to cross country schooling. In this case it is imperative that a young horse should be taken along and given confidence, and should not in any way be frightened. The cross country fences must not be flimsy or badly built, but well-built, solid and inviting. Ensure that the horse is not over-faced, otherwise he may put the brakes on and stop. Confidence comes from experience and the horse should never be put at risk.

Once the horse is well experienced at Novice level, some of the fences tackled during schooling could be of Intermediate standard. This can help the horse when he graduates, making the Novice fences seem easier when he is back in competition. When the beginning of the event season is near, aim to get some cross country schooling in (in good time before the first event), to remind the horse how to jump into water and how to tackle fences that are more solid than the show jumping poles with which he may be more familiar. Do not, however, leave this final schooling until the week of the event, as if the horse hits himself, inflicting bad bruising or a deep cut, he could be out of action for the first event.

Loosening Up

Like a finely tuned athlete, a horse needs to loosen up before schooling. There are different ways this can be achieved and you need to remember that variety is important to a horse, to prevent boredom setting in. My own horses will be hacked out before doing dressage or (in appalling weather) lunged. If they are at all prone to stiffness they are then worked on a long rein, and do trot and canter work until they are sufficiently loosened up to enable them to do more concentrated work. Often, at home, the horses are lunged over trotting poles to loosen their shoulders and to encourage them to establish more rhythm in their trot work.

If the weather is particularly bad in the early part of the season and a long freeze sets in, it may be necessary to go off to the beach to canter. Care needs to be taken as sand can be patchy, soft in some parts and firm in others. It is advisable to take the work slowly and gradually. While you are there, let the horse walk in the sea – the salt water is good for leg problems, acting as a coolant, and at the same time going through water makes the horse work.

Swimming in the sea might not be possible, but this exercise is extremely good for the horse. Many racehorse trainers now subscribe to the belief that after sore backs, shoulder injuries and lameness, swimming helps to bring the horse back to fitness. The exercise takes the weight off the horse's legs, but like canter work it must be built up gradually. There are good and bad swimmers among horses just as there are among humans, and to start with only one or two circuits of a pool are recommended. The exertion can be gauged by the horse's breathing. This exercise should only ever be done under the expert eye of a trainer.

Other Factors to Consider

Bear in mind that as the horse is being worked back to fitness his condition will change. Horses can often run up light during training and this means that more bulk food should be applied to the main feed. In contrast, other horses find it difficult to lose weight and this means that the amount of hay being fed should be limited and care should be taken to ensure that the horse is not eating his bedding – this can also be a common cause of colic. If he is eating the bedding, the horse should be stabled on newspaper or wood shavings. If the horse is becoming tense or excitable, this might be the result of too much work or of his not eating properly. Where this is the case, resort to slower work, and this should bring the horse back to eating properly.

If it is at all possible the horse should be turned out for an hour each day during preparation. Most horses benefit from their hour of freedom outside in a fenced-off paddock, where they can quietly graze. Mine are turned out in rotation for an hour every day and it seems to make them more relaxed, being a welcome break for them from being stabled all day.

Only when you feel that you are prepared and fit enough to do justice to your horse, and that the horse is ready, fit, properly trained and showing confidence and trust in his rider, are you ready to go eventing.

The Event Itself

The first important step is to map out the programme for the horse, deciding how many events you are going to enter in each season and where and when. Send the entry forms off in plenty of time with the required money and, assuming you are not balloted out after close of entries, you should be on your way.

If you have to withdraw from an event, make certain you do so before the closing date so that your entrance fee will be refundable. After the closing date the organisers will keep the money as another entrant could have competed in your place. The schedule of events gives in bold typeface both the closing date and the date of the competition. If a horse is being withdrawn at late notice, make sure you notify the organisers of the event as early as possible (at least two days prior to the event), as this helps their administration.

Travelling to the Event

On the night before the event, telephone the event Secretary's office to establish the times for the different phases. If it is a long way from home it is a good idea to enquire about the weather and ground conditions. Work out all the details in terms of travelling, including the route to be taken and the amount of time that should be allowed. If it is necessary to stable away, check the schedule for details (the stabling forms will be sent to you with the entry). More often than not stabling will be offered at a private yard or a local racecourse. When staying away you should always travel prepared for any eventuality, and this includes taking blankets, straw, water and feed. You should only put everything on the box the night before leaving if it can be locked up – tack is very expensive and should be kept safe at all times. Whenever the box is being prepared, check every item against the check-list, which should be kept permanently in the horse-box along with the flu vaccination certificate.

On the morning of departure, get up early and give the horse a normal breakfast. Groom the horse properly and plait the mane, ideally trying to get as many plaits as you can that look neat and are consistent in size. While doing this you can go through the dressage test in your mind so that it becomes firmly fixed. Remember to pick out the horse's hooves and to bandage carefully the legs and tail before loading on to the box. Ensure then that there is plenty of water for the horse to drink after the competition and also for you to use to wash him down after cross country. If there is any doubt about cancellation due to bad weather you must ring the Secretary or organiser for confirmation. There is nothing more frustrating than driving for over two hours, only to discover on arrival that the event has had to be cancelled because of snow or water on the ground.

Walking the Courses

When you arrive at the event try to park where allocated. If you can, get the numbers, check the times and present your vaccination certificate for checking on arrival, so much the better – this gets the administrative worry out of the way. Your first task will depend on your time of arrival and on the intervals between the phases, but it is very important to walk the show jumping course before this phase begins. Ideally, I try to walk both the show jumping and the cross country courses upon arrival. I usually walk the show jumping course first, as this is normally erected by 4 o'clock the previous afternoon, and I normally do this twice. Always establish the solidness of

the fences and the ground conditions as these will determine how the course should be jumped. If you see that the fences are flimsy and the ground is going to cut up then you know even greater care will need to be taken in approaching the obstacles and in having the right balance and impulsion.

When walking the cross country course it is important to stop long enough at each obstacle in order to determine the route you are going to take through it, where to make the approach, the precise point of take-off and where this is going to take you. In some cases you may need to consider an optional route, depending on how well the horse is going at the particular stage of the course. The essential is not to get caught in two minds or to change your plan of attack half-way round, as this often leads to an error – indecision can result in a costly mistake. While going round the course assess what is likely to happen to the ground after a number of riders have been over it, and how this might affect the take-off and landing sides at each fence.

The Dressage Test

Once the two courses have been walked you need to prepare both your horse and yourself. This means changing into the appropriate clothes and having the horse tacked up. You will need to follow your own plans on how best to work-in your horse, whether they involve lunging for a period before riding or simply going for a hack to loosen up the horse and familiarise him with the location and ground conditions. If there is a long time before the test the horse may be left tacked up, but you must ensure that he is warm enough, with blankets over the saddle and hind quarters. Use the waiting time to watch other competitors doing their tests. This will not only help you to remember the test, but will also enable you to establish how the ground is riding in the arena and whether it is on a slope or level. If the arena appears to be very slippery, this could affect your choice of studs.

When preparing the horse for his test always allow sufficient time in case the excitement of competition has made him fresh. Different horses require different amounts of time to get ready for their test. This can be as little as twenty minutes or as much as one and a half hours, depending on the ground conditions, the weather and the horse's fitness and temperament. Do not do or ask too much in the outside area but rather keep the horse moving, concentrating and interested.

Find out the numbers of the two horses before your test and when the first of these goes into the arena, get into the habit of taking the boots off your horse. If you do not have a groom or supporter the dressage steward will sometimes do this for you, if you ask nicely. Remember to drop your whip, or hand it to someone to look after while you are doing your test, and do this well before you are due to go into the arena. Make sure that you take the horse close to the markers, the white boards and the cars in which the judges will be sitting. In this way the horse will become accustomed to the sounds and the sights prior to doing the test and there should be nothing surprising for the young horse to shy at. The only other distractions that you cannot always be prepared for are the sound of the horn of a car in an accompanying arena, a horse getting out of control or

misbehaving in the next arena, the sight of horses going cross country or the sound of the tannoy. When going past the judges' car it does no harm to acknowledge them – smile and say good morning – but the important thing is to keep the horse moving all the time in a nice balanced trot. When the horn goes, enter the arena on the horse's best rein.

At the end of the test after the halt and salute, pat the horse. Then move off at a walk on a long rein. Once you are out of the arena make a fuss of the horse, giving it a handful of grass and a reassuring pat. Having collected the boots and your whip, either walk or ride the horse back to the box, and, when he is back at the box, change his saddle and bit ready for show jumping (if applicable), and put the rugs on to keep him warm. Do not forget to put the appropriate jumping boots on him.

The Show Jumping Phase

Once the horse is ready, and if there is sufficient time, leave him and walk down to the show jumping arena to watch a few competitors jump. This observation will quickly establish where the problems lie, which are the difficult fences, which are flimsy and likely to drop if touched, how the course is riding, where the distances between fences are proving awkward and what angles and turns will be best for the right approach. Again, 'ride' the course with two or three competitors to ensure that you have the order of jumps firmly established in your mind.

If there isn't time for this, take the horse down to the jumping practice area about twenty minutes before show jumping. This will give you time to watch some other competitors and also to loosen up the horse. When the horse has loosened up, ask someone to put a cross pole up and jump this a couple of times to get the horse used to jumping again. Then erect a low upright with a ground line. Jump this several times and then continue to jump a parallel. If the horse is jumping well this practice should be enough. If the horse knocks a fence in the practice arena this can often have the helpful effect of making him respect the fences more.

Be ready to enter the arena as soon as the previous horse has gone through the finishing line; trot round the arena, checking that all the fences are up properly and well into their cups. If you are not happy about a fence, ask the arena party to check it to make sure it is in its cups. When the bell sounds get the horse going at the speed at which you intend to jump the course – never go before the bell. If you are not sure, check, or wait for it to go again. Remember that when you have finished you must leave the arena mounted and to dismount will result in elimination. Do not leave the arena without your hat on – if you have dropped it, a member of the arena party will pick it up and give it to you. Do not dismount to pick up either hat or whip and, should you fall, remount before leaving the arena.

At the end of the show jumping, pat the horse and let him relax. If you have the time between phases walk down to the scoreboard, check the dressage scores and try to assess where you stand in the competition. At some events the dressage and show jumping scores are put up very promptly, and this means that before going cross country you know what time you need to do to be in with a chance of winning. If you are leading after the first two phases, work out how many seconds you have in hand as this may mean you can save your horse cross country, being able to go a little slower.

The Cross Country Phase

After the show jumping, prepare the horse and yourself for cross country. You will need to wear a back protector under your cross country sweater, and your number on top. Put the bandages or boots plus overreach boots on the horse's legs and then leave the horse tacked up and warm in the box. Take him off the box twenty minutes before the cross country and walk him down to the start, where there will be at least one, if not two, solid practice obstacles. These should be jumped so that the horse realises what he is about to undertake and that these are solid fences.

Enter the starting box a few seconds before scheduled departure. The starter will count you down and this is the time to start your stop-watch. Note that the time is taken from the time the starter says go and not from when you leave the box. If you make a false start (going earlier than scheduled), you will be called back, the time will not be started again and valuable seconds will be lost. Ride with purpose to the first fence.

If possible, before setting out you should try to get some feedback on how the course is jumping and where there may have been problems. By listening carefully to the tannoy, or by talking to other riders down at the start, you can often get an impression. This may help you determine whether you take the bold approach or the more time-consuming alternative at a particular fence.

At the end of the cross country course

Fig 119   Back protectors are recommended wear for the cross country phase.

the horse should be slowed down gradually, with the rider maintaining position and balance, and keeping contact on the reins. The reins should not just be dropped, losing contact, nor should the rider just sit down heavily on the horse. These are the characteristics of a poor rider. Do not stop abruptly at the end as this can cause leg damage. Once the horse has slowed down, dismount and then walk him slowly back to the box. Keep him moving until he has stopped blowing. After the cross country phase take the tack off the horse, put on a sweat sheet or rugs (depending on the weather), and wash him down, at the same time check-

ing for any bruising or abrasions which will need to be treated with coolant or an antiseptic spray. Make sure the horse is properly bandaged and walked. Give a little water and then feed, and make sure the horse is warm.

Throughout the competition, at the end, and in the days after the event, you should praise and encourage the horse. Remember, the horse is an animal and is not a mechanical machine. At best the horse is your friend and comrade, and at least a partner who needs respect, trust and confidence. If the horse goes well over an obstacle, pat and reassure him. After the final halt in the dressage phase,

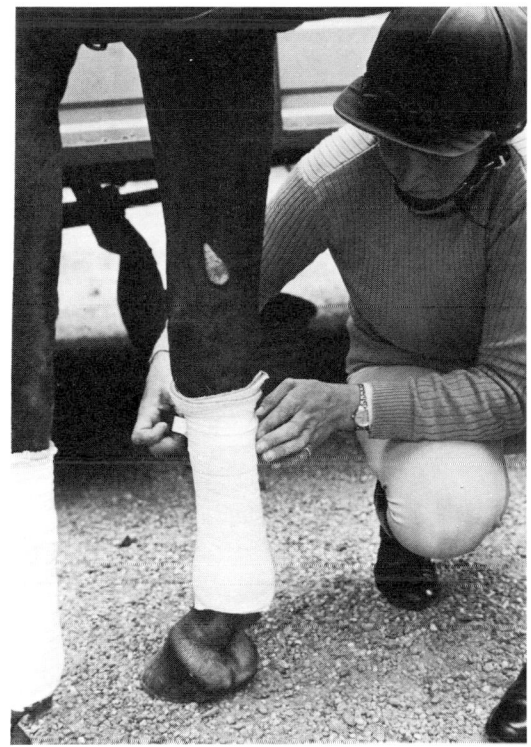

Fig 120 Securing the bandages for cross country with tape at the top.

and even prior to moving off in walk on a long rein, pat the horse's neck. Don't ignore the horse after the event is over but show affection and concern for his well-being. Over the days immediately following the event spend time with the horse walking or grooming, and checking fully that there are no ill-effects following the exertion. On the day after the event have the horse trotted up to check that he has come out sound. A happy horse that is cared for is noticed by everyone, while an unhappy horse that is not looked after and cared for properly can all too often develop a mean streak, or just appear dull, difficult and unco-operative.

Superstitions

Finally, don't worry if you are super-stitious – many competitors are, and indeed it is not uncommon in other sports. Footballers believe in omens such as coming out on the pitch last or putting their boots on in a particular order. I have always been superstitious. I never pick up a glove if I have dropped it myself; never wear green on competition days; never wear anything new at an event; always try to avoid wearing number thirteen or numbers that add up to thirteen (though there is little you can do about this) and I always wear something pink as it is my lucky colour – my cross country jersey is pink and I normally wear pink socks. Don't get paranoid about omens and superstitions, but smile about it after-wards. The main thing is that at the first event everything should be going the right way. A good, confident and well-prepared first event, that goes according to plan, will give you so much confidence that you will have just the right platform to build on for the future.

After the First Event and Beyond

Results and Prize Giving

If you are involved in the prize giving at the end of the competition, you must be correctly dressed, according to the stipu-lations laid down in the rules book. Basic-ally this means you should wear your jacket, breeches, boots without spurs and your hard hat. As a mark of respect to the sponsors who have generously supported the event prize giving should always be attended by the rider, or (only

Fig 121   The horse and rider ready to go cross country.

in exceptional circumstances) by one of the rider's entourage. Usually, a representative from the sponsoring company will give out the prizes and rosettes. If for some reason you can't turn up for the prize giving in person, then as a courtesy the Secretary should be informed of the reason for non-attendance, enabling him to assign somebody to stand in. There are normally only three acceptable reasons for not attending:

1.   Injury to horse or rider.
2.   A long drive home and a late prize giving ceremony.
3.   Preparation of, or riding, another horse at the allotted time of the prize giving.

Always remember to collect your dressage sheet before leaving the event or dressage competition. The judge's remarks are often very constructive and helpful, pointing out where the horse and rider need improvement, as well as where the test went well and badly. Over time, it is also useful to gauge what particular judges are looking for from a test as this can help when encountering the same judge on another occasion. Often it is the ability to gain every possible mark that can prove to be the difference between winning and being out of the places. When you see the sheet, read it through carefully and go through the test simultaneously in your mind; decide whether your impression and that of the judges agree. It is never sensible simply to throw the paper into the nearest dustbin in disgust with the judges as the chances are that the same people will reappear at another event where you compete. Bear in mind that the judges have given up their own time and are often expected to judge for long hours. They are also knowledgeable, so be grateful to them for their comments which are often constructive. It is far better for you to accept their viewpoint and learn from it for the future.

The sheets are usually accurate and checked in the Secretary's office, but it is never a bad idea for you to check your scores yourself, especially in a tight competition. If there is a disagreement, report it immediately to the Steward, asking politely if the scores could be rechecked.

When and if the event has been enjoyable, well organised and helpful to the progress of horse and rider, write and thank the people involved. A simple courtesy such as a letter is much appreciated by the Secretary or organisers since it recognises the efforts they have made to run the event with great care, concern and consideration for horse and rider alike. More often than not this has involved as many as fifty to sixty unpaid volunteers being briefed and organised properly. Don't only thank the organisers at those events where you win, but show your appreciation at any that you felt were well run and successful for the participants.

Keeping Records

When you are back home, write up a report (either that evening, or at least the next day, while it is still fresh in your mind) on how the partnership went. Lift the comments from the dressage sheet, and add your own asides about the attitude and performance of both horse and rider in the show jumping and cross country phases. This is a valuable exercise for three reasons: you will want to assess the horse's improvement over time and have a record of his competitions; should you come to sell the horse you will have his record fully documented for the purchaser to review; finally, it is a good way of keeping the horse's points score up to date so that the right campaign can be planned and the horse's progress controlled – this should ensure that he does not upgrade too quickly if he proves to be successful.

The basic rule in Britain is that a horse may only compete in the Novice Classes up to and including twenty-one points. If a horse is entered for a competition after the closing date, providing he has not had four outright wins he may partake without having to go *Hors Concours* (being a non-scoring competitor). In Britain a new Novice Class has now been introduced, called Novice Special or Novice 2, where the range of points is usually from 15 to 30. Check the individual events as the points spread can vary from one event to another, but in general this is an excellent class for a horse that has recently upgraded. It gives the chance for the horse to perform an Intermediate dressage test and Intermediate height show jumping course, while going across a Novice cross country course.

At the higher levels a horse who has over 60 points upgrades from the Intermediate level to the Advanced. It is recognised that many horses are not good enough to compete at this highest level and therefore there is the highly popular Open/Intermediate classification at many of the events.

Work After the Event

After the first event the amount of work to be done before the next will depend largely on the gap between competitions. Immediately after an event, however, rest is prescribed. After his first event the horse should be given a day of rest, and the next morning he should just be walked out and trotted to ensure his soundness, given a ten-minute walk in hand, and then allowed to graze in a field for an hour. He should be checked over very carefully for any bruises, abrasions or heat in the legs, and this should be carried out for the first two days as some injuries take time to come to light. On the second day after the event the horse should do only slow work normally constituting an hour and a half's slow hack, but by the third day he should be ready for work again and can be schooled. On the fourth day a canter can be undertaken, and on the fifth perhaps some show jumping. If the horse is a Novice and is competing fairly regularly, the sixth day could involve a light hack with the next competition on the following day. Even at Novice level you should not do more than two or three weekends in a row without giving the horse a break. The key is to watch the horse's condition, appreciate how much each event takes out of the animal and how quickly he recovers, and acknowledge the fact that wear and tear shorten the horse's competing life. You need to strike a fine balance for a Novice – he must gain the experience, but too much must not be demanded of him.

If there is a two day event in the plans for the Novice horse, ensure that he has been schooled over steeplechase fences at least once, prior to going to the competition. This is as important for the rider as it is for the horse. Bear in mind that the speed will be slightly faster than for cross country (670m per minute as compared to 540m per minute); as such, when practising, take a stop-watch and measure the distance to be covered. When training for the steeplechase phase, practise over an open ditch and two straightforward steeplechase fences, while maintaining the gallop in between, so that the experience is similar to that encountered in competition.

At Intermediate level and beyond the recovery time given to the horse needs to be much longer. The strain on the horse is considerably greater at this level, especially if he has been in contention throughout or if the ground conditions have been either very hard or really testing. If the horse is being aimed at a three day event then it is recommended that two, and a maximum of three, one day events are used as the preparatory run-up to the main event. A horse that is aimed for a three day event in the spring such as Badminton, Bramham, Punchestown, or Windsor will need to have a lengthy break after the event, sometimes as long as two months. Two three day events in one year are normally enough for a horse, although some people will do more. Again, the decision should depend on the horse and his speed of recovery, the preparation before the events, and the level of fitness achieved. Do not, however, do too many more as this will inevitably increase the chances of injury, with the horse being more likely to make a costly mistake through tiredness.

On those weekends when the horse is not eventing he will benefit from shows or dressage competitions, depending on his experience and temperament. Some horses become dull and uninspired with too many competitions while others thrive on work, and this is something that only the trainer and rider can gauge. When a horse is tense, relaxation and rest are the best cure. You should never increase the work-load believing that this will cure the problem. Instead, think about turning the horse out into the field for a break (or at least for an hour every day) and then introduce some slow hacking so that the horse comes through the tension. Often this situation arises because the team involved has failed to appreciate that a horse has to recover, not only from the event itself, but also from the mental anguish of being stabled away from home and from the physical exertion of travel. A young horse suffers even more than an older one from travelling and the experience of new places, and this alone can often result in him becoming dull and unhappy with a loss of sparkle. It is also fairly common for a horse to get over-excited at events, especially if he sees these as competition days with the chance to gallop cross country. To avoid this the horse should be taken to dressage and show jumping competitions during the event season so that he does not anticipate galloping cross country every time the horse-box drives out of the gate. This will help to keep him settled and make for greater concentration.

When and How to Compete?

With their older horses the Americans set a better example than most Europeans, tending to run them far less regularly, and in many cases for only part of the year. It also helps that their events are not timed in the same way as in Britain where competitors in contention are forced to go that much faster every time. Perhaps the competition for honours and selection is tougher in Europe but it certainly does not benefit the horse to have to give the maximum effort every time.

The more experienced riders in Britain have learnt about conserving their horses and Virginia Leng's approach to one day and three day events has proved to be both prudent and successful. Horses like Priceless and Night Cap II (both now retired), were never expected to gallop at the speed necessary to get inside the time allowed for a one day Advanced event. Instead they went at three day event speed, sometimes incurring time penalties in the one day event, but seldom, if ever, across country at a three day, where the time allowed tends to be slightly more generous. Similarly, the really top riders nearly always lead, or at least are amongst the leading contenders, after the dressage, and expect to show jump well. They do not, therefore, always have to go fast cross country to secure their placing. In some cases they may even have time in hand.

Upgrading

Over the years there have been many examples of promising young horses at Novice level who never came through to the Advanced level, because they became over-faced, were asked too many questions and were not schooled properly. It is not clever to gallop a Novice horse flat out around the course, hitting a number of fences and jumping others badly, finishing inside the time but in bad style. This is where the advantage of having private owners, or owning the horses yourself, rather than riding for an over-ambitious sponsor, comes in. Private owners tend to be as involved with the horse's well-being as the rider and will give the horse all the time necessary to fulfil his potential and the owner's expectations. Many of my good horses have not competed at Novice level until they were six, and before then many miles have been covered in hunter trials, hunting, cross country schooling and Pre-Novice competitions, let alone in the countless dressage and show jumping competitions. When the first event comes, both the horse and rider are ready. Should the occasion prove too much, the horse should be quietly schooled round the course so that the experience proves to be a relaxing and enjoyable one. A horse cannot be rushed, and if the foundations are not solid then the further the horse goes on the less likely he is to be able to withstand the pressure and complexities of the more difficult courses.

It is for this reason that many top riders deliberately avoid upgrading their horses too quickly. The Novice events are good experience, and when 20 points or four outright wins can take a horse out of this level of competition, it becomes imperative to devise a plan of campaign. Many of my horses have even been restrained when in winning positions at Novice events, in order to gain more experience of competition at this level, with different terrains and a variety of fences in varying weather conditions. There is no gambling involved so no one is being adversely affected by my decision not to go all out for a win; the key is to build up relevant experience for the future. There is ultimately no substitute for competition to gain this experience and to establish the horse's relative strengths and weaknesses, especially when he is being compared with other horses of a similar

standard. Learning how to jump a wide range of fences at sensible speeds and in the right way means that, when a horse is asked to accelerate, he can take the fences without any lack of confidence.

When you are competing and you move on to partake at an Advanced level, the horse will be required to carry a minimum weight of 75kg (165lb). This means that lighter riders will need to carry a weight cloth with lead in it. While it is important for the horse to get the feel of carrying the extra weight, you should not train extensively with it. He should have at least one jumping session to get used to the added weight. When racing trainers do their gallop work they always put the lightest lads up so as not to wear the horse out, saving the weight-carrying task for the race itself. More weight puts added stress on the joints and limbs, especially when the horse is travelling at speed. So, it is advisable to hack out and also to give the horse a jump wearing the weight cloth to get the feel of it, but you should not overdo it. The weight should be distributed evenly and as far forward as possible towards the withers and in front of the rider's legs. Horses carry the weight better here, and as little as possible should be either behind the rider's leg or in the back of the weight cloth. The horse will also be required to carry 75kg (165lbs) when you decide to compete in two or three day events.

Two and Three Day Events

Between Phases

When you are doing a two or three day event make certain that you are fully prepared. Ensure that the ten-minute break between the roads and tracks phase and the cross country phase is used constructively. Have your helper standing by in a predetermined place in the box with all the necessary equipment at hand – the right sponges, a bucket of water to wash the horse down, a scraper to remove the excess water, spare studs, shoes, bandages, tape, first aid box and over-reach boots, as well as a coat for the rider and, depending on the temperature and weather on the day, a rug for the horse. There should be a drink at hand for the rider and on a wet day a dry pair of gloves should be readily available. Bear in mind when riding in after Phase C (the second stage of roads and tracks) that there is a vet standing by; trot in smartly – this can save time since their task is simply to stop the horses that they consider to be unsound, to prevent them exacerbating any injury by going cross country. Each horse is different and if yours is excitable it may be sensible to leave the tack on, rather than taking everything off and then having trouble tacking up again. The important tasks to carry out are washing the horse's mouth out, washing down the neck and, on a hot day, putting cold water (or ideally ice) on all the pulses to reduce the body heat temperature. Conversely, on a cold day keep the horse well covered and don't allow him to stand around getting a chill during this ten-minute break.

Timings

Your first two or three day events can be confusing and difficult and, as such, you should make sure that the timings are clearly understood between each phase. The order is:

Phase A	Roads and Tracks
Phase B	Steeplechase
Phace C	Roads and Tracks
Phase D	Cross Country.

The timing given for A, B and C is based on the steeplechase being completed in the optimum time of two and a half minutes for Novice, and four minutes for Intermediate and Advanced. What can happen is that a rider who completes the steeplechase in a time faster than the optimum thinks that Phase C can be taken in a slightly more leisurely fashion. This is not the case – the time saved on the steeplechase has to be deducted from the time allocated for Phase C since this starts as soon as the steeplechase ends. For this reason, experienced riders, if they are unsure how quickly they have completed the steeplechase, aim to get back to the box at the end of Phase C with a minute or two to spare in order to be safe.

Veterinary Inspections

Remember, too, that there are regular veterinary inspections at three day events as a cautionary measure to prevent over-ambitious riders competing on unsound horses. If you miss, or are late for, the veterinary inspection you will be immediately disqualified. The stages to remember are: firstly, there is a vet's inspection the day before the dressage. At this inspection horses are required to be well turned out, plaited, with hoof oil applied and wearing a bridle and not merely a head collar. While walking around waiting your turn (inspections are done in numerical order) your horse should wear a rug. When called the rider or groom, looking tidy, should take the rug off and walk the horse up to the panel of ground jury and vet, stand correctly in front of them and await their instructions to walk or trot.

The second inspection is in the box before the cross country when the veterinary judge will check on the soundness of the horse after the endurance of steeplechase and roads and tracks. The rider must make sure the vet is satisfied and this may necessitate trotting the horse up before setting out across cross country.

The final stage comes the day after cross country when there is a morning inspection. The horse will be expected to trot up past the ground jury and vet and back again, prior to competing in the show jumping phase later in the morning or in the afternoon. The show jumping in the morning usually only occurs if a large number of entrants turn out for the final phase. The lower-placed competitors after the second day will complete their show jumping in the morning session.

After an arduous second day many horses will be stiff the following morning, and in this case they may need to walk or hack out for an hour before the vet's inspection in order to loosen up the limbs. It is important to walk the horse continually prior to inspection. You should not stop, as this can lead to a horse stiffening up or having the chance to feel his bruises – walking keeps him moving in a relaxed way. If you are unhappy with the soundness of your horse, you should withdraw before the inspection. Masking an injury, and forcing the horse to go on to show jumping just for that moment's glory, could destroy him for ever. In the World Championships at Gawler, Tinks Pottinger, on her splendid brown gelding Volunteer, was in a commanding position after a good dressage and a brilliant cross country round, only to be rejected by the veterinary panel and not allowed to partake in the show jumping. This sadly cost her the individual gold medal and also the team gold medal for New Zealand. However, at Burghley in 1987, Tinks was placed highly on both Graphic and Volunteer after spending the season in England.

The End of the Season

Finally, at the end of the season do not just turn a horse out immediately after the last event has ended. Wait until you are absolutely certain that the horse's legs are free from injury, that he is relaxed and calm and has fully recovered from the season's exertions. All too often people have turned a horse out on his own in a large field with a cattle grid, thinking the animal was totally tranquil and relaxed, only to encounter disaster as the horse galloped recklessly. It is much better to let the horse down gradually, checking on his legs, well-being, movement and condition. Slowly change the feed from high protein and start by letting the horse out in a small, safe paddock for a short period of time. If the horse is being roughed off, only remove the rugs and blankets after a few days as a tired horse can easily get a chill through lack of mobility, especially on sharp damp evenings in the late autumn before he has grown his winter coat.

10 The Fun of the Sport

Despite all the recent sponsorship money that has come into eventing it is still an amateur world, largely supported by people in love with the sport and not interested in financial reward. There is, of course, prestige attached to a sport that receives royal patronage in Britain, where the Princess Royal was European Champion on Doublet, and where so many of the events are in the parks or grounds of stately homes owned by the National Trust or landed gentry. This draws the more up-market sponsors and followers, and those seeking to be seen to be knowledgeable twice a year – at Badminton in the spring and at Burghley in the autumn. It is also a sport that tends to attract those who are better off financially as it is not cheap to compete, especially if the rider has a string of horses at different levels, a horse-box with living quarters for lengthy journeys or the two and three day events, and grooms, stabling and training to pay for. Fortunately, there are still a large number of children who come into the sport with dreams of emulating their heroes and who enjoy strong parental support. Many of them, if they retain their enthusiasm and have natural talent, eventually make the grade.

For all this, the sport, in Britain at least, retains its traditional and distinctly conservative nature. The administration at Stoneleigh, the Horse Trials Groups centre (a subsidiary of the British Horse Society), has changed little over the years and, while recognising the need for commercialism, prefers to play down this aspect. The rules are based on etiquette, correctness and the discipline of both horse and rider; and the organisation of every registered or affiliated event is strictly controlled by Stoneleigh. The stewards and judges give up their time freely for the thrill of the event and only receive travel expenses and subsistence, normally constituting a coffee and light luncheon supplied by the event organisers. The fence judges at every single cross country fence at each event are unpaid and are normally local volunteers who have an interest in the sport, either as spectators or through family connections with competitors or organisers. Without all these contributors, who give up their time so freely and readily, the sport would die on its feet – each event needs many committed volunteers.

As I have tried to point out in this book, eventing is not a sport to be undertaken lightly, least of all if you aim to compete effectively. It requires dedication and patience, and a huge investment in time and effort to get results. There will be many ups and downs, trials and tribulations, hopes and expectations shattered and fulfilled, triumphs and disasters. All are experienced over time and it is the bad times that will make you appreciative of success and make the sport worthwhile. Perhaps it is the realisation that things can so easily go wrong that breeds humility even into the most able of event riders. There is never a feeling of arrogance or over-confidence extended by the top names – they display, rather, hope, exhilaration and sheer enjoyment for what they have achieved to date.

To compete seriously you need a minimum of two horses, so that you have a back-up if something goes wrong with your lead horse. When I was on the short list for the team for the Olympics in 1980 with Castlewellan, I had William Hinckling as a strong back-up. If both horses are going well at the same time, the rider can choose his events carefully and ensure that he gives the horses sufficient time to rest and recuperate. You need a good groom or stable manager, unless you have the time to look after the horses, ride them and get them ready at shows and events, just relying on a family supporter. Ideally, the groom should be able to ride so that the walking and hacking work can be done for the competitor. It also helps the rider to have a colleague watching progress, setting up fences, doing the lunge work and going with the horse-box to competitions. Without some company the close season can seem to drag by, and the sharing of competitions with someone else who is closely involved is missing.

Most riders start by having family support and by treating the sport as a hobby during school holidays and weekends. When it becomes a way of life, only the most dedicated of parents can remain the owner of the horse. I was particularly fortunate in that my father has been very much involved with the sport. This meant he actively encouraged me when I left school at fifteen, and over the years his excellent eye for a horse has provided me with good mounts, and the opportunity to compete. Often my father will go off on his own, look at a horse and then I will also see the horse before I

purchase. Importantly, he has organised his business commitments and extensive work-load, both at home and abroad, around the competitions and he has seldom missed an event in this country, irrespective of mileage or the weather. The fact that my cottage and the stables are situated next to his house has helped him to retain his interest in the sport. His comments and appraisals on the horses and riders under my jurisdiction are considered, perceptive and usually accurate. Indeed, when I was injured and not at home much from 1981 to 1984, I suspect my father missed the horses and the competitions every bit as much as I did.

Over the years I have ridden for owners other than my father and been fortunate enough to have fun ones. A good owner is one who has a keen interest but tends not to interfere; someone with whom you can be honest and someone who is patient, accepting the highs and lows and enjoying the sport; and someone who does not view the involvement as a commercial enterprise. If you are running a yard and turning over horses, or even just producing good young horses or riders with their own horses, an owner helps with a contribution to the overheads. They can also help in that they often live miles away, operating and living in a different world with a different circle of friends, detached from the horse world. All this gives you an outlet away from the sport for a short spell and a different viewpoint on life. All my owners have also been great friends and I have never fallen out seriously with any of them. You must treat owners with respect, involve them in the plans for the future, discuss honestly the potential or shortcomings of their horse, seek their advice and make them feel party to any decisions through discussion of the options. Always inform them immediately after a competition (if they were not present) of their horse's fortune, whether good or bad. Invite them to all the competitions, giving them advance notification, and make them feel part of the team. Owners become dissatisfied when they feel they are being used simply to pay the bills, either being ignored or not involved. Good sympathetic owners are hard to find – if you have them, don't lose them.

In the end all that I can say is that the sport is there to be enjoyed. The friends I have made over the years have remained – pupils I have trained, people against whom I have ridden or fellow team members, have all provided me with fun, enjoyment and many happy memories. There is a bond between event riders and an important social side to the sport. It is the people in eventing who make it the enjoyable pastime it has proved to be for me. I hope this book will have helped increase your interest in, enthusiasm for, and enjoyment of the sport.

Conclusion

After twenty years in the sport of eventing I still get a buzz and excitement from competing and going to Horse Trials. Even now I find that I continue to learn and I still have lessons myself. My 'instructors' help and the back-up of my father and my staff and of many owners and their good quality horses has meant that I can still compete effectively.

Today, I am able to put something back into a sport that has given me so much fun and such a wonderful way of life. I train young riders and bring on young horses and am proud to have had, in the last four years, three riders in successful Young Riders and Junior British teams. Furthermore, I am now privileged to be on a number of selection panels and committees concerned with the betterment of the sport for the future. Additionally, my experience and lessons learned have brought me into the world of judging, where I am an FEI International Judge. My judging commitments have taken me to many three day events, including Kentucky and Radnor in the USA, Punchestown in Ireland, Brador in Holland, and Burghley, Windsor and Chatsworth in Britain, as well as engagements in South Africa and Jamaica. This has benefited my own riding, especially as I move into the more advanced spheres of competitive dressage.

Still, there is nothing to surpass the thrill and challenge of riding, seeing young horses improve and fulfil their potential and getting places in hotly-contested Horse Trials. This still remains the ultimate fun of the sport.

Appendix — Registration and Administration

In order for a horse to compete at any event that is recognised by the authorities he must be registered. The rider, too, has to be registered to compete and given the training required it is also advisable for the rider to have registered to compete in dressage and show jumping as well as at trials. This means that the rider can quickly register a horse to compete at affiliated dressage meetings or partake in show jumping at a show. It is extremely important for the horse and rider to compete in the specialist spheres to assess progress and evaluate their potential. The views of experts on the performance of horse and rider in these respective disciplines can help enormously, as can having someone tape a round of show jumping or a dressage test on video. Too few riders in Britain bother to join the dressage or show jumping groups believing they are 'eventers through and through'. I have always liked to compete against the best to assess my progress and, indeed, enjoy trying to beat show jumpers at their own game and to win qualifiers in major dressage competitions.

When registering you will automatically receive the rule books, lists of judges and the qualifications for competing in different classes and at different levels, as well as a schedule of competitions. The rating of horses in show jumping is based on money won, while dressage and horse trials are based on points. It is absolutely essential, when buying a horse, that he should be checked out carefully to ensure he either has the points claimed or does not have any. If the horse is not registered under rules then the name of the horse can be changed, but if he has competed and has points he must retain the same name under which he has already run.

When competing, the horse must be at least 15 hh. and five years old before he is allowed to do a Novice event. This is to protect the horse as there is always the danger of an inexperienced or unknowing competitor seeking to push a young horse before he is mature enough to be able to cope with the disciplines.

As you start to compete, keep a very close eye on the number of points gained by each horse, as you can all too quickly jump him out of a class. The problem with this is that, on the one hand, you want a horse to be ready for an event and so be able to give a good account of himself on the day, but at the same time he will need the experience of miles on the clock at Novice level. At the Novice level he only needs twenty points, or four outright wins, to be upgraded and yet, for a young five-year-old, more time at the Novice standard could be critically important. Many good young horses are pushed along too quickly and asked too many questions before they are ready to negotiate them. In some cases horses are moved through Novice and Intermediate levels to Advanced in a single year. In other cases, horses are asked to do too many events in a given period. It is my hope that rules will be introduced to protect horses from having to do more than a certain number of events, especially three day events, in a season.

With my young horses I like them to go well from the start. If the ground and weather conditions are not suitable for a horse's first event, I would wait until later in the year before commencing, especially with five year olds. The older horse, being more mature, would be able to cope better with adverse conditions.

If a horse is travelling abroad he will require a passport that clearly establishes his age, his colour and any distinguishing markings, and his breeding. This, again, must travel with the horse, otherwise he might be refused entry. In some countries there is also a lengthy quarantine period, or there might be strict rules on where the horse can go.

It is a good idea to have established contact and a reasonable relationship with the governing body, as this can help in areas of doubt or at times of dispute. Furthermore, try to be understanding and courteous to the organisers of events as they are often doing the work voluntarily – remember, they are the life-blood of the sport. Keep them on your side – it can only help you and boost your enjoyment of the sport.

Further Reading

The Event Groom's Handbook, Jeanne Kane and Lisa Waltman (Event Books International / Threshold Books Limited)

The Event Rider's Notebook, Mary Rose FBHS (Harrap Limited)

The Horsemaster's Notebook, Mary Rose FBHS (Harrap Limited)

The Event Horse, Sheila Willcox (Pelham Books Limited)

The Athletic Horse, Carol Foster (The Crowood Press)

The Riding Instructor's Handbook, Monty Mortimer (David & Charles)

The Manual of Horsemanship, The British Horse Society and the Pony Club (Threshold Books Limited)

Up, Up and Away, Lucinda Green (Pelham Books Limited)

Regal Realm, Lucinda Green (Methuen)

Index